D0481193

"Rao provides a fascinating deconstruction of the factors, mindsets, and habits that must all combine to create an unmistakable life."
                                        —Cal Newport, author of *Deep Work*

"Several years ago, I got a request to go on Srinivas's podcast. It was a small show then but in the years since, I've seen it grow into one of the biggest and best shows around and watched the creator become a bestselling author and an inspiring leader. How did he do it? By following the exact 'unmistakable' formula laid out in this book."   —Ryan Holiday, author of *The Obstacle Is the Way*

"This book is a wonderfully concise collection of insights from edgy thought leaders mixed with Rao's own personal narrative. His struggles, his breakthroughs, and his relationship with surfing, as a sanctuary and a metaphor for inspiration, will inspire you in turn to tap into your own unmistakable work. Congratulations, Srinivas, for writing a soulful, poetic, and accessible little book."   —Erik Wahl, artist and author of *Unthink*

UNMISTAKABLE

WHY

ONLY

IS

BETTER

THAN

BEST

SRINIVAS RAO

PORTFOLIO / PENGUIN

PORTFOLIO / PENGUIN

An imprint of Penguin Random House LLC
375 Hudson Street
New York, New York 10014

ISBN: 9781101981702 (hardcover)
ISBN: 9781101981726 (ebook)

Printed in the United States of America
1   3   5   7   9   10   8   6   4   2

Designed by Alissa Rose Theodor
Set in Charter ITC Std

To the thousands of people from around the world who have tuned in to listen to the show every week.

This book is for you.

CONTENTS

UNMISTAKABLE

For the first ten years of my career, I followed a script and played by the rules. I graduated from the University of California at Berkeley. I collected bullet points on my résumé as I aimlessly wandered from one job to another until I had been fired from nearly every one. I applied to graduate school to collect yet another societally approved badge of honor, my MBA, because I thought maybe this choice would lead to something great.

By the time I finished graduate school, the era in which competence, convention, and conformity guaranteed the path to a safe and secure existence was over. The jobs once reserved for freshly minted MBA graduates were gone and never coming back.

The consequences of being simply competent have turned the careers of many people into cautionary tales. When we're merely competent, the value of our work is diminished until it can eventually be outsourced to the lowest bidder, making us a dispensable commodity.

The future belongs to individuals and organizations who are unmistakable.

I define the *unmistakable* as art that doesn't require a signature. It's so infused with your heart and mind that no one else could have created it. It's immediately recognizable as something *you* made—nobody could have done it *but* you.

Now maybe you don't identify yourself as an artist, but I define art as any creation: a project, interaction, blog post, report, paper, book, song, performance, company, and so on. When we view our work and the world through the eyes of an artist, we can't help but see things differently.

An unmistakable person, whether a poet or a painter, a podcaster or a YouTube star, does what he or she does in a completely distinctive way. You couldn't write a job description for what the unmistakable person does. You might be able to describe the work, but the core value is impossible to replicate or mimic. No course, blog post, or how-to book can teach you how to become this person. The art of being unmistakable is difficult to achieve, yet it is one of the most effective traits of an artist, a business, or an individual.

So why does it matter if nobody could have created it but you?

When you're the only person who could have created a work of art, the competition and standard metrics by which things are measured become irrelevant because nothing can replace you. The factors that distinguish you are so personal that nobody can replicate them.

When Malala Yousafzai speaks, her message is unmistakable.

When Toni Morrison writes, her voice is unmistakable.

When Slash plays the guitar solo to the Guns N' Roses song "Sweet Child O' Mine," his timing and technique are unmistakable.

When Danny Meyer starts a restaurant, the service is unmistakable.

When Banksy paints, his style is unmistakable.

When Lindsey Stirling plays the violin, her virtuosity is unmistakable.

Unmistakable people make a dent in the hearts and minds of humanity. They create a ripple beyond any measure.

As I neared the end of my MBA at Pepperdine in 2009, I was faced with two choices. I could either continue on the tried and true path, which I knew would lead me only to a dead end, or I could gamble on an uncertain quest that could lead me to disaster—or discovery. I had taken the first path all through my twenties to end up at this unhappy destination of thirty.

As I started to examine the choices I had made over the past decade, I realized I had never been proactive. I'd always chosen from the options that were put in front of me. I'd settled over and over again. I settled for the first job offer I got. I settled for doing work that didn't mean much to me. I settled for the best I thought my life could be as opposed to thinking about and going after what I really wanted.

If I wanted to end up in a drastically different place by the age of forty, I'd have to make drastically different choices in my thirties even if they might be questioned, frowned upon, and misunderstood.

When I started my career, I'd blindly signed the contract of society's life plan as if there were no other option, but now I was starting to realize that it was and always had been completely negotiable.

The first inkling of that realization came to me on December 31, 2008, after I had turned thirty and was on the tail end of a study abroad program in Brazil. My friends had all gone home early because they ran out of money, and I had become quite bored with sitting on the beach. So I decided to rent a surfboard and give surfing one last shot, after many failed attempts, before I returned to the United States. Standing up on a surfboard that day for the first time created a ripple effect of change in my life. When I returned to school for my final semester, instead of going to the bookstore when my financial aid check was deposited, I went to the surf shop to buy a surfboard and a wetsuit. I surfed on the mornings I didn't have classes, I surfed in between my classes, and I surfed every weekend.

Given that I had no job waiting upon graduation and I had depleted nearly my entire savings account, I realized I could seize this opportunity to effectively start from scratch. What I had was a blank canvas on which I could deliberately create a masterpiece, which would give me an opportunity to once and for all put an end to my crisis of mediocrity.

Midway through the summer after my graduation from Pepperdine, I started to see that surfing—which started as a way to pass the time—was now transforming into a way of life. On the days when it didn't get windy too early, I was in the water from sunrise to sunset.

When I stood up on a wave, every ounce of fear, anxiety, depression, and self-doubt didn't just dissipate, it vanished. Even though I was jobless, surviving primarily on peanut butter and jelly sandwiches and sleeping on the living room floor of an apartment that was once mine, for the first time in my adult life I experienced unparalleled joy. I went to sleep every night eagerly anticipating the waves of the next day. Every time I stood up on a wave, the doubting voice in my head lost its power over me. Surfers say that riding a wave is a bit like taming a wild horse, and it makes you feel almost superhuman. While my outer world appeared to be in shambles, my inner world was transforming, one wave at a time.

When surfing, there is no one but you and the wave. You're liberated from the expectations and standards of other people. Surfing is a performance in which you are the main audience, allowing you to connect with and discover your unmistakable self and process in the most direct way possible.

One summer afternoon, I was rinsing off my wetsuit near lifeguard tower 20 in Santa Monica, California, when I met a fellow surfer who was clearly older than me. I told him I was in the water so much because I'd just finished grad school and was struggling to find a job, and the only thing keeping me sane was surfing. He told me that surfing had gotten him through a terrible divorce, as well as through the death of his mother.

That day I realized I had stumbled on something truly magical, something that would forever continue to change my life, a love affair that I'd carry on from my first wave to the grave.

It would become the driving force of my creativity.

It would lead to meeting one of my best friends and my future business partner, Brian Koehn.

Being in the water became my essential daily meditation. It was a lifeline, a spiritual practice, and a central metaphor for everything else I would go on to do.

Each wave seemed to wash away the structures, beliefs,

and ideas that had been imposed on me since I was old enough to understand what I was being told. I started more and more to question the life I had meant to live, and the advice of so many well-intentioned people:

Stick to well-lit, straight and narrow paths.
Follow the rules.
Don't make a ruckus.
Don't ask too many questions.
Climb the corporate ladder.
Obey your elders.

This script, from my parents, teachers, mentors, friends, colleagues, and others, I took and followed to the letter. My results weren't average. They were abysmal. I'd been fired from every real job I'd ever had and never made much money. Worst of all, I'd lived a life that was completely devoid of meaning, intention, and purpose. Then I looked around and saw others trying to follow the same script to achieve success and noticed that they were just as miserable.

Throughout our lives, we inherit the limitations of society's expectations and conform to its ideals until they weigh so heavily on us that we stop questioning their existence. When these unspoken rules are imposed for long enough, they become the unconscious scripts that dictate our lives and trap us in an invisible prison. We become so indoctrinated, it's as if we've been institutionalized. We forget that our life is what we make of it. Only when we have the audacity to question the status quo can we disrupt it.

We forget we're free to dismiss others' expectations any time we'd like.

Remember: the door is always wide open.

If you walk out that door and abandon all the expectations society has laid out for you, the truest expression of who you are emerges. You play with abandon, optimism, and curiosity—like you did as a child. You begin a quest for which only you are made, the passage that only *you* are destined to make.

You learn the art of being unmistakable. But this doesn't happen in one brief moment, one blog post, one work of art. It's not something you do. It's not a technique, methodology, or formula. It's something that becomes part of your DNA, a lens through which you view the world. And once you see the world this way, it will never look the same.

When I started learning how to surf, I'd always get in the water with fear and trepidation because I had no idea what I was doing, and my big blue foam surfboard was basically a symbol of the fact that I was a kook (surf lingo for incompetent). Every morning I would look at the surf report in hopes that the waves wouldn't be too big. One wave at a time, countless hours in the water, and seven years on, I'm still learning how to surf. Some days still intimidate me. You never really stop learning how to surf.

My trajectory of learning to surf has been much like that of an artist or creator. It's been a process of letting go of fear, doubt, expectations, and the need to be perfect. It's been a process of commitment, risk, and embracing the possibility of a wipeout. And every time I go slightly past the boundaries of my comfort zone, my capacity for risk, for charging bigger waves with bravado, increases. Every small wave prepares me for a bigger one. I still wipe out on plenty of waves, but I've learned one essential lesson: the fear of wiping out never goes away until you've actually gone for a wave, and the fall is almost never as bad as you imagine it to be in your head.

Creating work that is unmistakable has been a process of letting go of all the masks that I've hidden behind my entire life. Every creation is like a wave, and with each piece of work I put out into the world I dare a bit more, I let the world see a bit more into the depth of who I am. I gradually increase my capacity for risk. I may say what other people are thinking but are afraid to say. I challenge the status quo or redefine it. I take bigger and bolder risks until I reach a new normal. I might fail. But as in going for a wave, the antidote to fear is to commit to the act of creating and to keep putting work out into the world.

Inevitably, surfing had to be the organizing principle of this book because the pursuit of waves has defined my life and my personal quest to become unmistakable. From standing on-shore to paddling out, from riding the perfect wave to wiping out, surfing parallels any artistic, entrepreneurial, or ambitious endeavor. Whether you're yearning to change careers or start a business, drop out or go back to school, figure out your artistic medium or fine-tune your art, my hope is that these pages will help you become unmistakable.

Surfing led me to start what has become the *Unmistakable Creative* podcast. Since then, I've interviewed more than six hundred people I call Unmistakable Creatives about their work and life process for my podcast. They explain what they think being unmistakable means, what they do to foster and nurture their creativity no matter what field they're in, and how they deal with the setbacks that come with the territory. They include best-selling authors such as Tim Ferriss and Seth Godin; inspiring practitioners like pastor and author Rob Bell, Basecamp cofounder David Heinemeier Hansson, and entrepreneur Danielle LaPorte; and geniuses you've never heard of, including a bank robber who became a talking head on the subject of the criminal justice system, a graffiti artist who writes business books, a painter who is completely blind, and world-class cartoonists who have become masters of their craft. I've synthesized their insights and observations together with my own lessons to offer you a springboard toward becoming unmistakable. I'm not offering you a roadmap or even a guide, because only you can plot your own course.

It's also not the science, it's the *art* of being unmistakable. Art requires you to attempt what hasn't been proven to work, and as author Todd Henry said, you must "be decisive in the face of uncertainty." There's no formula or set of prescripted instructions. The most unmistakable elements of your art come from intuition and instinct.

In any creative endeavor or goal worth pursuing there are obstacles. Sometimes you achieve those goals quickly and other times it takes longer than you'd like. You can read, prepare, and study until you're "ready." But "ready" is an illusion. You won't really know what to do until you're in the water. Opportunities are like waves. You can go for them or keep letting them pass by. But the sooner you go for a wave, the sooner your ride will begin. Like every wave I've ever ridden, every person's path is different. It will come with its own set of challenges, its own circumstances, and in its own time.

Surfing isn't only about riding a wave; it's about the Zen-like high and thrill that comes from it, known in surf lingo as "the stoke." The beauty of the stoke is that it can't be measured or quantified, because it's a limitless gift. When creation becomes its own reward, you'll transcend yourself. You'll be on your way to unmistakable.

My goal is that reading about what makes others unmistakable will galvanize you into getting off the sand and into the waves.

Let's go. Surf's up.

PART 1:
THE PADDLE OUT

Even though I've lived in California since 1993, I needed fifteen years and, ironically, to leave the country before I finally started to surf.

We often wait like this when it comes to the pursuit of some of our most important dreams. We drive by the water admiring it from the safety of our cars, or we simply stand onshore watching and admiring those who are already in the water. We justify not doing anything by convincing ourselves that people in the water have something that we don't. They've had lucky breaks that we never will, or they've won some sort of genetic lottery or happened to be in the right place at the right time. While in some cases this might be true, our justifications start to become excuses and then narratives we repeat that limit our potential.

When you start to pursue anything that falls outside the boundaries of societal expectations, anything that disrupts or disturbs the status quo, the sirens of safety and security will begin to go off like a fire truck blazing through the streets of New York City. A decision to disrupt the status quo is in many ways a decision to disrupt yourself and your life. But we resist changes like this, despite knowing how much a subtle or significant shift in our lives can come to outweigh what we fear.

And we fear that taking a plunge into the water, into the unknown, and doing the work required to become unmistakable will be worse even than the boredom or dissatisfaction that we currently feel with our lives. So we just stand onshore with our feet sinking into the sand. We continually choose to do nothing, settle, and compromise until we get to the end of our lives and find ourselves looking back at a life that could have been.

- *A life in which we could have published the novel we've stashed in our desk drawer.*

- *A life in which we could have started the company or nonprofit that is deep within the chambers of our heart and mind.*

- *A life in which we could have dared more greatly and dreamed more audaciously.*

But we *always* have a choice to take one small step forward to begin our quest for change. Nearly every innovative, groundbreaking, creative idea that defies the limits of what we once thought was humanly possible started as nothing more than a thought in someone's head, a moment of creative daring, before it became that person's unmistakable dent in the universe.

Given that we're about to enter a new and unfamiliar environment and attempt to learn a completely new way of living, we have no idea what our limits are. We might imagine those limits to be greater than they are, dreaming of being Michael Jordan when we've never picked up a basketball in our life. Or we might imagine them to be worse than they are, that we can't even try to write or draw, sing or dance.

Inevitably, when you get in the water you'll face obstacles

like rocks, waves crashing down on your head, jellyfish, and other surfers yelling at you. Similarly, the pursuit of unmistakable work also comes with its own set of obstacles that you will have to face, like critics, naysayers, moments of panic, fear, anxiety, self-doubt, and competition.

Before you get ready to paddle out, consider what's making your feet feel like they're stuck in the sand forever.

SHARKS, DROWNING, AND OTHER THINGS THAT KEEP YOU FROM GETTING IN THE WATER

Two forces, one external and the other internal, are the most common culprits that account for the delay and death of many potential projects and the failure to pursue our unmistakable art. To become unmistakable, you have to become aware of these defeating influences and how they work, so you understand their power to work against you and know how to assess or ignore them.

The Voices of Parents, Peers, and Society

When you start to become unmistakable, the voices of people who want you to follow *their* plan will get *really* loud. Those voices will often come from well-meaning friends, family, and colleagues, and some less-than-sympathetic adversaries like competitors, critics, naysayers, and strangers on the Internet.

Whatever their intention, these voices will question your sanity and say you've lost your mind. They'll give you a list of reasons why you will fail, and tell you how the odds are stacked against you.

For many years, I heard some variation of the following:

You don't have enough experience.

You just don't have the talent.

You're too old.

You're too young.

Your cousin or friend or uncle or aunt tried to do this and failed.

If this doesn't work out, you'll be old and broke. Then what are you going to do?

How are you ever going to make money doing that?

Nine out of ten businesses end up failing.

Only one in a thousand people will make it in acting, writing, or anything creative.

Millions of blogs are out there. Why would anybody read yours?

This is such a waste of your education.

Friends and family will fill your ears with tales of woe, disasters, and debacles. They'll kindly suggest a backup plan that involves following the script that they follow, what society has told them to do. They'll tell you that your work is no good and they'll question your talent.

Why do the voices get so loud?

1) People want you to remain as you are because you make them realize they're ignoring their own calling. People are uncomfortable when you start to change, because your actions remind them what they've been avoiding in their own lives. They're forced to confront the fact that they're choosing to remain the same while you're making a drastic shift in the direction of your life. You hold a mirror up to all the fears they've given in to and all the goals they've chosen not to pursue.

2) **Criticizing is easier than creating.** If you're a critic you get to avoid the risk of failing, looking stupid, and making the world wonder what the hell you were thinking. As a critic, you're off the hook. But the most iconic creators in history have all contended with critics. Every single book, piece of music, or film has received negative reviews. Browse the contemporary reviews for classic books like *To Kill a Mockingbird, The Great Gatsby,* and *The Sun Also Rises*. You'll find a one-star review for all of them. If your work is unmistakable, it will have critics. So you must embrace or ignore the critics and create anyway.

3) **Some people are just rule followers.** Sometime early in 2013, I went to a job interview. One of the people interviewing me, Chuck, had become incredibly indoctrinated. When I asked him about the culture of the organization he said, "When we say work starts at eight o'clock, we don't mean eight-fifteen." I never forgot that. Following rules was his world. I quickly realized in that moment that this was not my world and I didn't want to be a casualty of defending the status quo as Chuck had. You can follow a set of prewritten rules or you can start to make your own.

The people who criticized me when I started have since moved on. A handful of critics have been replaced by thousands of people around the world who have supported my work.

If I had listened to those critical voices, I would never have put another idea out into the world.

You wouldn't be reading this book.

The *Unmistakable Creative* podcast wouldn't exist.

I would have missed out on getting a world-class education from some of the greatest minds of our time.

And I would be miserable.

The best way to silence your critics is with commitment, conviction, putting your head down, and getting back to work. The people you admire certainly didn't start out with legions of fans, readers, and supporters of their work, and they have dealt with their fair share of criticism. They're the ones who didn't let the critics paralyze them. You probably haven't heard of the ones who let one bad review destroy their art: they never shipped anything again, never used the opportunity to improve, and never offered the world their unmistakable art.

A former boss at a major market research company wrote me off as not interested in controlling my own destiny. What he didn't realize was that I was simply not destined for his version of what it meant to control destiny: climbing the ranks within those walls. My goal was to break down those walls, build, make, and create things that didn't yet exist. As Morgan Freeman said in the movie *The Shawshank Redemption,* "Some birds aren't meant to be caged." To me, a limitless opportunity for self-expression is an essential ingredient to controlling my destiny.

Author Robert Kurson, best known for his book *Shadow Divers,* was hardly destined for success when he was in high school. Because he was ranked 606th out of 660, a guidance counselor recommended that he not go to college, and instead apply for the Peace Corps and hope for the best.

Robert's love of storytelling, however, led him to write for his high school newspaper, and he eventually got the attention of somebody at the University of Wisconsin. He gained admission, earned straight A's, attended Harvard Law School, and became a best-selling author. Needless to say, if he had taken to heart his guidance counselor's advice, his life might look a lot different now.

Similarly, Mars Dorian, our special projects artist at the *Unmistakable Creative,* has had his work called too edgy and provocative. Plenty of people don't like his work. But if you've ever seen a book cover, logo, or piece of art he's designed, you instantly know it's his. He's the embodiment of what it means to be unmistakable, whether or not everyone loves his art.

More than twenty-six publishers turned down what became a giant bestseller, *The 4-Hour Workweek* by Tim Ferriss. Tim has since made a fortune as a start-up adviser and investor, he hosts his own podcast, and recently he was the star of his own television show called *The Tim Ferriss Experiment.*

Another spin on dealing with criticism comes from blogger and creator of Fearbuster.com Jia Jiang, who turned being rejected by every venture capitalist who wouldn't fund his start-up ideas into a global movement and a book, *Rejection Proof,* a hilarious examination of how to overcome fear and dare to live more boldly.

Every one of these people contended with critics, people who doubted them, and people who rejected their ideas. But they didn't let the sting of that criticism keep them from making the unmistakable contribution they were determined to put out into the world.

Remember that the sting of our critics or naysayers is often harshest in the moment. The temptation is to believe them and listen to what they have to say, but it stands staunchly in your way to becoming unmistakable.

When my previous self-published book *The Art of Being Unmistakable* landed me on TV with media pundit Glenn Beck, I was exposed to a significantly larger audience than I had been in my entire career. And it wasn't long before some vilifying reviews appeared on Amazon. The one-star review that is permanently etched in my mind reads, "I hope Rao is a better surfer than writer." In spite of the success I was experiencing, that criticism still hurt. And I knew that if I attempted to cater to my critics, I'd not only hold back, but lose my voice in the process. I haven't read a review since.

We also have to be aware of our negativity bias when it comes to the sting of our critics. Think of how easily you can let one small negative part of your day dominate an otherwise perfect day.

In his book *The Happiness Advantage,* Shawn Achor describes the positive *Tetris* effect. People who play the game *Tetris* for an extended period of time start noticing potential *Tetris* patterns everywhere (e.g., while walking down the cereal aisle in the grocery store). The same effect, it turns out, can be applied to positivity and happiness. The simple act of noticing three good things creates a positive *Tetris* effect in your life. So rather than focusing on the critics, you start to shift your focus to the handful of people who are supporting you, and suddenly you'll start to notice a lot more of them.

Another way to mitigate the voices of your critics is to create a picture of what your future would look like if you believed what they said. My business partner Brian Koehn described the crossroads he was at in high school: he could work a dead-end job like every other teenager or start his own company. He decided to start a skateboard company. Because he was still in high school, he had more than his fair share of naysayers. He visualized what would have happened if he had listened to his critics:

> *It felt like being told what to do, and I never wanted to be told what to do. I know where that path ends. But the skateboard company was a whole world of possibilities. The picture of the future was all around me: I saw my peers not making any money, not having any fun. I saw all these adults working jobs that they hated. I had this constant reminder that if I didn't take this chance that's exactly what my life was going to be like.*

If he had listened to his critics, Brian wouldn't have ended up touring the Midwest, pushing his limits, having insane amounts of fun, making money, and selling his skateboards in twenty-seven stores within two years. Whether he had started his company or not, the critics would have been long gone. If he hadn't started the company, their words would have continued to linger, affecting other decisions he made throughout his life.

When you visualize how much catering to your critics can limit the potential of your work, you can more easily ignore them and move on. Compromising and giving up on something that matters to you is a really high price to pay just so you don't have to hear those voices when you decide to go against the grain. Nobody will criticize you for maintaining the status quo—but you'll never be unmistakable either.

You have to find the courage to take action in the face of criticism if you're going to do anything unmistakable, and realize that your critics are not the ones who are going to live with the consequences of the choices you've made.

The critical voices are loudest when you're standing onshore, contemplating a paddle out. Once you're in the water, on your way to becoming unmistakable, the voices will gradually be drowned out by the sound of the surf. You've left behind the critics on land. You'll hear your own voice whispering that you are doing what you're destined to do. Nothing silences those external voices like catching a perfect wave while the gods smile on you and your heart races.

Fear, Resistance, and the Insidious Nature of Validation

To get into the water, to start making whatever art you feel called to make, you also must learn to deal with the *internal* voice of fear, doubt, and resistance. Critics' voices can be loud, but perhaps more intense even are our own voices. Think of all the companies that haven't been started and all the stories that haven't been told because of fear, resistance, and the voice in someone's head.

The voice in your head is harsher than any of your critics. If anybody else spoke to you the way you talk to yourself, you'd never tolerate it. And unlike your external critics, you can't block the voice in your head on social media, mark its e-mails as spam, or hang up when it calls. At least one day a week the voice in my head goes on a tirade that sounds like this: *You're never going to make it. This stuff is really coming out the wrong end. Why even bother?*

The voice takes every ounce of fear, self-doubt, and anxiety you have and, like a filmmaker adapting the words of a screen-writer, turns it all into a montage of the worst-case scenarios. You can fire the voice, and it'll be back at work tomorrow at eight a.m. sharp. You can slam the door in its face, and it'll walk right back through it. No matter how hard you try, there's no getting rid of it. It's a pain in the ass, a thorn in your side, a ruthless little bastard. You can hear it, but you can't see it or touch it so you can't beat the hell out of it.

The voice in your head is resistance, the lizard brain. As marketing guru and author Seth Godin describes, the lizard brain is in charge of fight, flight, feeding, fear, freezing up, and fornica-tion. In other words, it's hungry, scared shitless, anxiety ridden, and horny. Someone you'd probably never want to date, but are in a relationship with until the end of time. As author Steven Pressfield wrote in his book *The War of Art,* the voice is always lying and always full of shit. So why on earth are we so tempted to listen to it? Because it never shuts up. It talks nonstop. It has something to say about every single moment of your life, every single person you meet, everything you write. Perhaps you don't realize what your lizard brain is even up to; it's time to start paying attention to this unrelenting voice.

The movie *A Beautiful Mind*—based on the biography by Sylvia Nasar of Nobel Prize–winning economist and mathematician John Forbes Nash, Jr.—is a brilliant lesson on dealing with the voice in your head. Mathematician John Nash, played by Russell Crowe, suffers from schizophrenia and severe delusions, and learns that by his not engaging the delusions, they start to lose their grip on him. While they're never gone, when he doesn't speak to them, they quiet down. If you start to listen to the voice in your head, you might be astonished by what you're telling yourself and the subconscious narrative you've created. Like Nash, not engaging with that voice will help quiet it down and take away its power.

Motivational speaker Philip McKernan shared one of the most profound insights I have ever heard on managing your internal fear and voice:

> We all want to get rid of and eradicate fear. Therein lies one of the biggest problems. I don't think we ever deal with and put fear to bed. It's always going to be part of us. The problem is that we won't accept that. So we put on our sneakers, our Lululemon pants, and our Under Armour tops and we sprint and we run from fear. And eventually we have to stop and take a breather, or stop and take water, or sleep, or pee, or whatever the hell we have to do. And you turn around and the

bastard is behind you. And the bastard is fear. Fear doesn't need water. It doesn't need caffeine. It doesn't need sleep. It doesn't need anything. It will always be with us. So, do we want to spend the rest of our lives running from it or do we want to turn about and face it? Sit down, get to know it, process it. Then you don't feel you have to run away from it. You can walk this world with it. And it loosens its grip on you. And ironically when you embrace it as a natural part of your being it doesn't control you anymore.

Your voice wants nothing more than for you to get into an argument or dialogue with it. But if you observe it, ignore it, and start to do unmistakable work despite it, the voice loses whatever power it has over you. It may never shut up but it certainly gets much quieter. The antidote to the voice of fear is to put your work out into the world, little by little, day by day, until you can live with the voice, while also ignoring it. You overcome resistance drip by drip with seemingly small accomplishments, one at a time, until you find a capacity to dare a bit more.

I'd love to tell you that after posting hundreds of blogs, producing podcasts, and completing other projects, that voice is no longer in my head. In the process of writing this book, the voice tried to derail me every single day. But each time I sat down with less concern for the quality of what initially showed up on the page, I started to make progress. Using an arbitrary constraint, say a thousand words or thirty minutes, and a simple rule like "just keep typing," I'm free of the need for perfectionism. By committing to the *process* instead of to the *outcome*, I'm able to let go of my unproductive concern for quality. Inevitably I end up with a lot of words on the page, and some of them are good enough to keep.

The desire for validation feeds the hungry voice. If we're not aware of it, our desire for validation can keep us from getting in the water and going for a wave. In my Indian culture, people are usually validated by certain badges of honor: Ivy League degrees, graduation from medical school, and other conventional goals that are all part of a linear achievement-oriented path. When you decide to go down a road that has no guarantees and no clear success markers, you are forced to look for validation in a different way. The trajectory of my life has been anything but linear—yet I still wanted my parents' approval. I didn't realize quite how much until I was walking through Central Park with author Jonathan Fields and said, "Now that I've gotten a book deal with a publisher, I hope my parents won't think I'm just screwing around on the Internet." He laughed and said, "It's funny how that still matters, isn't it?" And while my parents *were* proud, I realized that the issue was mine. They could never say enough for me to feel that my work mattered. My need for their validation was a bottomless pit.

We have more opportunities for validation today than ever before, which keeps the addiction alive:

- *The number of "likes" we get on a status update.*
- *The number of followers we have on Twitter.*
- *The number of people who read our blogs.*
- *The number of compliments we get in any given day.*
- *The number of our bank balance.*

If we follow these seeming tokens of validation, we let the voices of our validators dictate the choices we make, even though they aren't the ones who will live with the outcomes of our decisions. We do our work in service of the people we'll never be enough for, as opposed to the people who are already rooting for us. Our work becomes safe and manufactured—and a lot less unmistakable.

Discussing criticism and validation, Donald Miller writes in the book *Scary Close* about being paralyzed by potential criticism as a by-product of his success:

> *I'd sit at the keyboard with their criticism in my head and include so many caveats in a chapter that the words no longer had flow. And worse, I'd have people's praise in my head and be terrified I'd never live up to their expectations. . . . I'd achieved a little success and suddenly there was something to lose. And there was an expectation to meet too. It was paralyzing. Suddenly there was a risk to just being myself.*

Donald came face-to-face with the desire for validation that increases when we get the slightest taste of it. Validation may temporarily boost our egos, and inflate our vanity metrics, but to produce unmistakable work while in need of it is artistic suicide. I've written blog posts with perfectly crafted headlines, sanitized and optimized to be shared by as many people as possible. Without exception, for every single thing I've created while looking to be validated, the level of validation has fallen short of my expectations. On the other hand, when I've written something without the desire to be validated, the piece succeeded not only by external measures (in my case, traffic and book sales), it also was more authentic, and had a much more significant impact on the people it reached.

Validation is like a drug. The more we depend on it, the higher dosage we'll need for it to work. When it's gone, we'll experience everything that we would with a drug withdrawal—darkness, loss, pain, and the unquenchable desire for more.

The most useful piece of advice on validation I've ever received was from my business partner Brian Koehn: treat support as one of the environments you live in. Realistically we all need validation, so instead of searching for it everywhere or from people you know you can't get enough of it from, be deliberate. Choose two or three cheerleaders, people who support you and will give you the amount of validation you need for your work. Brian is one of mine, who seems to find the little bits of genius in just about everything that I produce. My good friend Charmaine Haworth, coach and speaker and another one of my cheerleaders, has the superpower of making people feel their best when they're at their worst.

Another way to validate yourself and your work is to change the way you measure your success. Rather than relying solely on numbers, I started to measure meaning. I created a simple Evernote file where I keep stellar iTunes reviews of the podcast, every tweet that made my day, complimentary e-mails, and more. On the days when I question whether my work matters at all—almost every day—and when I can't quiet my internal negative voice, I look through that file instead of Google Analytics.

LAND LESSONS

Surfing lessons don't begin in the water. They start onshore. During a land lesson, a surf instructor attempts to simulate the experience of riding a wave by having a student lie down on a stationary surfboard on the sand and go through the sequence of paddling, pushing herself up, and landing on her feet. The instructor will repeat this sequence multiple times before the student decides she's ready to get into the water.

A land lesson is a perfect metaphor for our tendency to fall into paralysis by analysis. Many people get stuck by constantly looking for the next guru to solve their issues or the next blog post, podcast, course, or conference that will be the answer to all their questions. They make the mistake of assuming that if they're prepared enough, everything will go smoothly and they won't wipe out. If all you do is read this book and decide not to do anything else, you've effectively chosen to stand onshore and watch people surf. You watch others fulfill their unmistakability while you prepare and wait.

Admittedly, jumping into the water can be scary, because once you get in the water the land lesson becomes fairly useless. Getting yourself up on a stationary board on the sand and doing it in moving water are very different things. When you get into the water, all sorts of variables exist that don't on land: Waves, big and small. Other surfers. A board tied to your feet that can hit you in the face when enough force is behind a wave. White water, reefs, rocks. Water that's sometimes shallow and sometimes deep.

But take a deep breath. Paddling out into the water and surfing is worth it, and learning the mechanics of surfing, or your unmistakable endeavor, is simply the first step. When a friend asked me how you learn to read the waves, I said, "You spend a lot of time in the water." That often means you have to be willing to start before you feel ready.

The very first incarnation of what is today Unmistakable Creative.com was one interview as an individual blog post on another Web site with a link to an MP3 that people could download. I talked too much during the interview, kept interrupting my guest, and the work was a pale precursor of what it is today. My Web site has literally gone through thousands of iterations and a significant metamorphosis to become unmistakable. But I needed to start with that first step of getting in the water.

The first time I published an e-book and tried to sell it, I didn't know what I was doing. It wasn't well edited. I made a lot less money than I was expecting. You could say it was like catching a first wave. I didn't ride it perfectly, but I went for it.

Learning from books, podcasts, courses, and conferences is fine. But if you don't transform knowledge into wisdom—the by-product of action—you're stuck in a perpetual land lesson. Any creative project or endeavor will always have unknowns. At some point you have to get in the water and go for a wave. You'll take a few waves on the head and wipe out, but as surfers know, you need only one good wave and you'll be hooked.

GETTING IN THE WATER

Something brings each and every one of us to the shores of unmistakable work. Maybe you've been fired from every real job you've ever had, feel lost and miserable, and are desperately seeking a drastic change in your life. Maybe you're fed up with playing by the rules, living your life according to a script, devoid of meaning, adventure, intention, and purpose. Maybe once and for all you're committed to living *every* moment of your life deliberately. Whatever it is that's brought you to the shores of unmistakable, it's time to grab your board and get in the water. The unmistakable truly begins with a decision to get in the water and go for a wave.

As surfers stand on the shore feeling excitement, anticipation, and possibilities, they evaluate the conditions:

What's the wind doing? What are the trends?

How big are the waves? What is the opportunity at our disposal?

How crowded is the lineup? What does our competition look like?

Assessing the conditions is about awareness. It gives us a sense of what we're up against, the obstacles in our way, and what we'll have to bring to the lineup in order to do our most unmistakable work. While the conditions are always changing, if we completely ignore them, we're liable to find ourselves out at sea in a storm that we're going to drown in. Unmistakable work doesn't happen in a vacuum, and without an awareness of the conditions, we're likely to mimic and replicate what already exists, attempt things we won't succeed at, and create work that is the antithesis of unmistakable.

Paddling out parallels the start of unmistakable work. When we write the first words of a book, put the first drop of paint on a canvas, share our Web site with the world for the first time, or develop the first screen of the user interface on the app we're building, we paddle out. You might be able to look at the market, find a niche that isn't too crowded, and time everything perfectly. It's possible you'll spot a trend and be at its forefront. It's equally possible you won't see an opportunity. You'll be forced to experiment, fail, repeat, act in the absence of clarity, and wait for an opening to reveal itself.

As you evaluate the conditions, you might notice a perfect place to paddle out, a channel, or a moment when the water is calm and you can get to the lineup easily. You might manage and time the paddle out just right. But so many of these variables are up to the whims of Mother Nature. They are always changing and out of our control. The one thing we *do* control is our decision to grab our boards and get in the water. When we focus on what we control, it gives us power over our lives and our work.

You will always have days when you arrive at the shore and the conditions are absolutely terrible. But seven years of surfing has taught me one really important thing. If you're not willing to show up and occasionally get in the water on the days that suck, you won't be able to reap the rewards of the days that don't.

Six years ago I plugged a microphone into a laptop to begin recording conversations with bloggers. My goal was to find out how they had managed to grow their audience. I had no idea where it would lead. I was paddling out without knowing even what kind of wave I might catch . . . or if I'd catch a wave at all. Evaluation of the conditions indicated that there was not much of a future in what I was doing. In fact, experts were saying that podcasting was dead. But conditions have changed significantly since, with journalist Kevin Roose writing in 2014 that "we're in a golden age of podcasting." I showed up when the conditions sucked, and because of that I've reaped the rewards of a time when they don't.

So our evaluation of the conditions can sometimes be misleading because they're always changing. Certainly when conditions are treacherous with hurricanes and thunderstorms, paddling out makes no sense. Similarly unwise would be to invest money for your mortgage in a whim or attempt anything if your downside is bankruptcy, jail time, or death. But between these boundaries, play! We often imagine false conditions that stop us from plunging into the water.

Waiting for the right idea and the right wave at just the right time has caused people to spend a lifetime standing on the metaphorical shore of their dreams. Speculation has never been the catalyst for turning ideas into a reality. You can spend a lifetime planning, preparing, and attempting to perfect your ability to stand up on your surfboard while you're on land. But if you're on the shore for too long, preparation eventually turns into procrastination. The first time I took a surf lesson, the instructor said something to me that I think is a fitting metaphor for our temptation to stay onshore. I wasn't grasping quite how to stand up on a surfboard, and we had spent more than an hour on land.

He said, "You know, a kid wouldn't have tolerated an hour-long land lesson. They would have insisted we get in the water." Right after that we got in the water. It's time to leave your outer adult onshore, and let your inner child paddle out to surf.

Maybe you're waiting . . .

Until you have more money.

For a break, like winning the lottery or getting "discovered."

For permission.

For reassurance that you won't take a wave on the head and wipe out.

For a moment when you have enough confidence, enough courage, and enough hubris to believe you're something special.

For when you just "know" the right direction to take or realize the big project you should start.

For a mythical date in the future when all of the above are true.

Nothing you're waiting for will happen while you're on the beach. Unmistakable happens in the water, riding waves and making art.

Leap Before You Look

Victor Saad's early life was rough. His parents divorced while he was in high school, after emigrating from Egypt. However, a group of youth pastors, teachers, and coaches provided him with a sense of direction. He saw in them a glimpse of who he wanted to be. Despite the common path of becoming a doctor or engineer in his Egyptian culture, Victor decided to pursue a career in education.

While working with middle school and high school students, he helped develop a student center in suburban Chicago. Saad decided that his next career move would involve combining business and nonprofit education.

After studying for the GMAT, and realizing how high tuition would be, he opted out of applying to business school. In an effort to find an alternative to a high-priced MBA and design his own master's degree, Victor Saad started a blog and educational initiative called the Leap Year Project: eleven different internships over the course of a year, with a TEDx talk as his graduation. He reached out to technology companies, ad agencies, and other organizations, and worked on a project with each of them. He then launched a Kickstarter campaign and published a book called *The Leap Year Project*.

But his work was far from over. He was left with the question of whether or not he could replicate the Leap Year Project in a way that would disrupt higher education. The result was a whole new way of educating people called the Experience Institute, which two graduating classes have been through so far. An array of industry leaders advise students and help establish great opportunities within their field of study, and a plethora of host companies support students in their efforts. The Experience Institute has joined forces with Stanford's design school, and Victor has appeared on *Forbes*'s "30 Under 30" list.

Victor had no way of knowing how this would turn out when he started. He just got in the water and kept going for waves, one internship after another. In a conversation on the *Unmistakable Creative* podcast, he said, "I could see it but I just couldn't figure out how to get there."

When we're starting anything, we can often see the end we have in mind, but have no idea how to get there. Only through taking action, experimenting, and leaping into the unknown do we start to see what's needed to reach our goal. With each step forward the view changes, our perspective expands, and we see things we couldn't see or know before. Even if we fail, sometimes it's taking two steps back that causes us to take twenty forward. Failures provide us with feedback about what we did right and what we did wrong, and enable us to correct course. With each wave we go for, we learn more and new insights are revealed. Our capacity to ride each wave with guts and grace grows.

Until you get in the water you won't know how well you can surf. You have to not only embrace the unknown, but be willing to suck, and keep making your art or working at your craft until you don't. You learn to bring color into your life.

Vision Without Sight

Like so many of my podcast guests, John Bramblitt had a difficult childhood. By the time he was two years old he had severe epilepsy. His health problems continued throughout his childhood and into high school with numerous hospital visits. John turned to visual art as a way of dealing with his challenges.

Then in 2001, while he was in college, he lost his eyesight due to a seizure disorder.

The loss of his eyesight forced him to learn how to do everything, like walking, cooking, and reading, in new ways. He had to navigate the world using touch as his primary sense. Again, he turned to the visual arts, a seemingly odd choice for someone who is visually impaired. He developed painting techniques that employed touch, using varying paint textures to create a landscape so he can feel his way across a canvas. The first time he painted blind, he literally could not see what was on the canvas. He had no idea if it would work or not. Years later, he's established a successful career as an artist. At an art gallery opening, somebody approached John and asked him to identify the artist—and was stunned to learn it was John himself. His paintings are infused with such a wide variety of colors and realistic images portrayed in such vivid detail, it's hard to believe that he's blind.

DEFINING MOMENTS AND INTUITION

December 31, 2008, was the tail end of my six-month study abroad in Brazil. Up until that point I'd never managed to stand up on a surfboard. I had made something like fifteen attempts to surf and taken a lesson or two. I had paddled out but never caught a single wave. That day I decided I was sick of sitting on the beach drinking. So I rented a surfboard from a rather unsavory Argentinean guy who looked a bit like Aerosmith lead singer Steven Tyler, except significantly older. After twenty minutes in the water I was able to stand up and ride a wave to the shore. To say that it felt like a religious experience is an understatement. That moment divided my life into before and after. I thought it was a fluke, so I tried to catch a second wave and I stood up again. By the time I had to return my board, I had stood up so many times I had lost count. When I got out of the water, it was as if all the years of stress over the jobs from which I'd been fired, the relationships that hadn't worked out, and my chronic health issues were gone. I felt such a lightness. I thought, "I want to feel this way all the time. I will make decisions accordingly."

Defining moments like mine can change the trajectory of our lives—but only if we acknowledge them. Mastering the art of being unmistakable means learning to trust your intuition when you experience a defining moment. We tend not to trust our intuition enough to act on defining moments because we're so caught up in doing what we think we "should" instead of what we feel we "must," and so we bury those moments or disregard them. It took a really long time for me to learn both how to recognize these moments and how to trust my intuition.

Unfortunately, I think that the way we learn to trust our intuition is by not trusting it. Unless you're a New Age hippie blessed with the intuitive gift of always being right, great wisdom is the by-product of doing lots of stupid things:

- *Taking the wrong job*
- *Dating the wrong person*

- *Trusting people you shouldn't trust*
- *Living your life according to someone else's expectations*

You have to eat shit on a lot of waves to figure out which ones are worth going for.

My first year out of college I had two job interviews. One was at a company that seemed to really have it together, and another was at a start-up where a friend worked. On the drive to the latter, a medical transcription software company in Milpitas, California, I'd already made up my mind to go with the first company. The only reason I agreed to the interview was as a favor to my friend. My intuition was screaming, "This is a disaster in the making." My future boss seemed like he had cut his teeth selling ice cubes to Eskimos. The environment was completely sterile. When I was offered positions at both companies, I foolishly chose the start-up because of an extra $5,000 in salary and the fact that my friend worked there. I thought I "should" take the job. Turned out, my intuition was spot on. Three weeks after I began, the start-up cut pay across the board by 20 percent. Every few weeks the CEO went on a rampage and fired someone. It was such a toxic work environment that I developed a severe case of irritable bowel syndrome.

The IBS is a good example of how not listening to your intuition can have unintended consequences, including a direct impact on your health. Danielle LaPorte, author of *The Fire Starter Sessions: A Soulful + Practical Guide to Creating Success on Your Own Terms,* shared a story in an *Unmistakable Creative* episode about how a certain CEO makes business decisions. If the CEO's meal goes down well during a meeting, it's a yes. If the meal doesn't go down well, the deal doesn't happen. If your body is on the fritz, that's likely your intuition on red alert. Listen to your body.

Fear made executive coach Suzannah Scully take a corporate job that she knew in her bones was wrong for her. In an interview on the *Unmistakable Creative*, she said, "I've done that many times in my life, that 'should' path. And every time it turns out poorly." According to Suzannah, "The universe first gives you a whisper, then a shout, and then a two-by-four to the head." Out of fear, most of us wait for the two-by-four before we trust ourselves.

When we don't trust our intuition, we say yes to things to which we should say no. We live our lives according to other people's expectations. We make choices out of our need for validation as opposed to what gives us a sense of fulfillment. We end up wearing layers and layers of masks until we've quietly blended into the fabric of society, as we subtly defend and accept the status quo. When we trust our intuition, we say yes and it feels right. We have an inner knowing, an unwavering conviction and commitment that what we're doing will ultimately lead us to somewhere better.

For Ryan Holiday, author of *The Obstacle Is the Way* among other books, going against conventional wisdom to drop out of college was a defining moment. He could see a future that would open him to other possibilities, although he couldn't know the specific details of that future. Because he trusted his intuition, he was able to work with some of the absolute masters of the craft of writing and marketing like Robert Greene and Tucker Max. He went on to write several books, work as the director of marketing at American Apparel, and become the marketing mastermind behind many best-selling authors.

In 2009, I recorded and posted a conversation with a blogger named Josh Hanagarne. When we were finished, he said, "Don't underestimate where this is going to take you." A few months later, I interviewed my thirteenth person, another blogger, Sid Savara. Afterward, he wrote to me:

> *You should go full speed ahead on the blogger interviews— and really dedicate yourself to it.*
>
> *I think your interview series would be extremely successful if you made a completely separate blog for it. Your personal development writing and the other people's guest posts are good, but the interview series—man! That is the stuff that *really* sets your blog apart. You've got a huge opportunity with those interviews though—*nobody* I know of is doing in-depth audio interviews like you as frequently as you—and, I like the style of your interview. The genuine interest you have in the other bloggers and their lessons really comes through, and that makes the interviews much more enjoyable to listen to. The interviews you've already done are like unfound treasures.*

An hour later, I bought a domain and mocked up the very first version of what is today UnmistakableCreative.com. I knew deep down it was something I had to do. I saw endless possibilities. I had never acted so quickly or with so much enthusiasm toward anything in my life. The difference between following advice and acting on intuition is that with the latter you feel inwardly, deeply compelled to do something, while the former feels as though it's being forced upon you. I could have written off Sid's advice as just another blogger on his soapbox, but I didn't. I recognized the defining moment and trusted my intuition. Doing so has opened up opportunities that I couldn't have planned or prepared for, leading me to create unmistakable work.

Likewise, when the author Steven Pressfield trusted his intuition, it paid off in spades:

> *I was starving as a screenwriter when the idea for* The Legend of Bagger Vance *came to me. It came as a book, not a movie. I met with my agent to give him the bad news. We both knew that first novels take forever and sell for nothing. Worse, a novel about golf, even if we could find a publisher, is a straight shot to the remainder bin.*
>
> *But the Muse had me. I had to do it. To my amazement, the book succeeded critically and commercially better than anything I'd ever done, and others since have been lucky too. Why? My best guess is this: **I trusted what I wanted, not what I thought would work. I did what I myself would find interesting, and left its reception to the gods.***

If Steven attempted to create something purely for validation, something he thought would work, as opposed to what he intuitively felt compelled to create, his work likely would have fallen short of all his expectations. It might not have succeeded commercially, and he'd be stuck with work that he didn't want to make in the first place.

However, every creator must take into consideration the delicate balance between art and commerce. To create something based on intuition that appeals to an audience outside of yourself is the unmistakable's goal—at least it should be. Ignoring the interests of your intended audience is what blogger Sonia Simone calls the "naked mole rat" approach. As she wrote in an article on Copyblogger.com: "If you start a blog on naked mole rats, it had better be for passion rather than profit. The audience that wants more information about insect-like collectivist rodents is going to be pretty limited."

One of the myths of trusting your intuition is that it will be blissful. Initially that may not prove to be true. If trusting your intuition were free of obstacles and challenges, then everybody would do it. Your intuition may lead to loss and heartache. In many cases the willingness to trust your intuition involves a decision to go through pain. But with that decision also comes the opportunity to experience the kind of character transformation that wouldn't be possible without pain. Trusting your intuition involves risk and the possibility that things won't go according to plan. Worst of all, that we are wrong and our critics will be validated.

But when your critics are silenced, and more important, when you experience the pure joy that comes from doing something that's truly unmistakable, the obstacles, the pain, and the criticism will all be absolutely worth it.

Unmistakable Creative: Elle Luna

Throughout our lives we have choices between what we feel pressured to do and what we feel inwardly, deeply compelled to do. When we do the first, we live our lives according to the expectations of others. When we do the second, we trust intuition and pursue a path toward unmistakable. We are choosing between what designer and painter Elle Luna refers to as "should" and "must."

The phrase "follow your dreams" is an overused cliché. But Elle Luna is the only one I know who quite literally followed a recurring dream she had until it led her to quit working with high-profile start-ups like Uber and Mailbox and pursue that dream. By combining her visual art, her words, and her message of The Crossroads of Should and Must, *Elle Luna has created an unmistakable expression of herself and her work. Today Elle works out of her studio in San Francisco, where she paints self-portraits and her nighttime dreams, designs textiles, and writes books.*

Elle's Defining Moment

Elle began to have a recurring dream, which she described in my conversation with her on the Unmistakable Creative:

> In my dream I would sit on the floor of this room—
> concrete floors, tall white walls, warehouse windows,
> and a mattress on the floor. When I was in that space,
> I would be filled with the warmest, most pervasive
> sense of peace and calm.

A friend then asked her if she'd ever thought to look for the dream in real life. While this suggestion bemused and startled Elle, she decided to pursue it—and ended up finding the exact room on Craigslist. She eventually found herself sitting in the same room in real life that she'd seen in her dreams:

> I looked around at the room and I began to wonder what
> was all this about? What was going on? Out loud, I asked,
> "Why am I here?" As clear as anything I know to be true,
> the room replied and said to me, "It's time to paint."

At the height of her career, having worked at the world-class design firm IDEO, on a team that redesigned the Uber app, and on the Mailbox app with more than a million subscribers prior to launch, she left it all to pursue her quite literal dream of painting in the white room.

Our defining moments, those in which we have to trust our intuition, don't always happen according to our specified time lines. They don't necessarily make logical sense. They *require us to trust that when we go for a wave and leap into the unknown we will manage to stay on the board.*

Elle's defining moment led to a profound revelation:

It was this moment that I recognized what I now call the crossroads of should and must. I was at the peak of a start-up and this fledgling bizarre expression of wanting to paint. Those worlds were both equally appealing, but they were totally different. I couldn't keep it up. I couldn't do both. And standing right there between those two paths, I had to choose. I looked at my finances. I saw that I could buy myself some time. I just went all in, two feet into painting, and that's what's led me to today.

Over and over, we arrive at this crossroads, our defining moments, and in those moments we're either walking away from a calling or going toward it. If we see the pursuit of our calling as the pursuit of a perfect wave, we're either walking away from the water or toward it, away from what makes us unmistakable or toward it. And this is the choice we get to make each time we arrive at the crossroads of should and must.

Redefining Positive Outcomes
and the Creative Process

The willingness to throw out work, and create work that was never meant to see the light of day, is essential if you're going to become prolific at your craft. My personal notebooks contain thousands of pages, hundreds of half-baked thoughts, and a plethora of incoherent ramblings that were never meant to be read. Elle applies a very similar process to her art. As she said, "Some artists give it a go on one try and do it all in one fell swoop and that's not me. I hope maybe one day to be there, but I still throw out tons of work and that's cool." If you get comfortable with throwing out your work, you'll get comfortable with making more of it.

After stressing about her first art gallery opening, Elle decided to stop to think about what a "good" outcome would look like for herself:

It would be people loving my paintings. But I reframed and realized that actually "good" was mounting a show of sixty pieces of new work in a gallery. That was it. That's all I had to do. So after we finished mounting the work, I looked around and thought, "I did it. I totally did it." When the people arrived, it was icing on the cake. What they thought didn't matter because my goal had shifted, and it was a much more important goal.

Often we define positive outcomes by things that we have absolutely no control over, like whether or not people love our work. But when we're able to reframe what a good outcome is, to dig deep into what it means for us, we're able to redirect that energy into the work itself, and increase the likelihood that the work will exceed our expectations.

Defining Unmistakable

Elle's definition of unmistakable is "when it comes from a place of 'must.' Work and action and intention that comes from that unavoidable place that's palpable: you can feel it, you can see it, and the work, design, words, images, are simply undeniable."

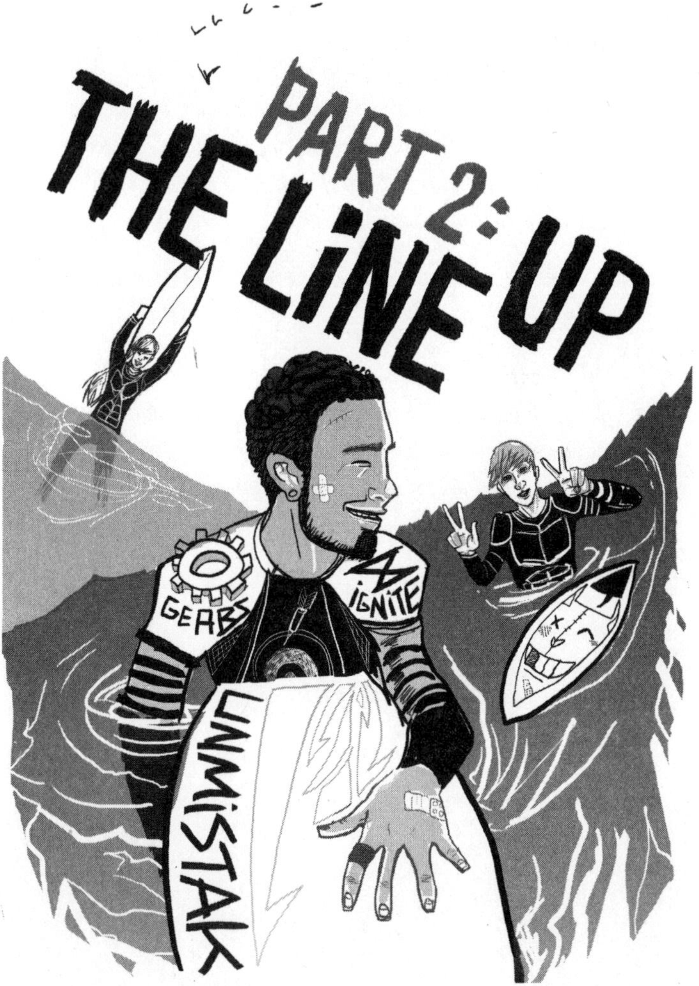

PART 2:
THE LiNE UP
GEARBS
iGNiTE
UNMiSTAK

Surfers in the water waiting to catch waves are referred to as "the lineup." If there's anything my local surf spot has taught me, it's that when the waves are good, the lineup will be crowded with people with more talent and experience than you. If you want to catch waves, you have to develop the necessary skills to stand out in the lineup and abide by surfing etiquette. Only one person can be on a wave at a time, and the ratio of surfers to available waves is almost never ideal. As a result, opportunity breeds competition, and people with the necessary skills to stand out end up with the highest wave count.

Similarly, creators have more opportunity at their fingertips than at any other time in history, with the gap between creativity and technology closing. Without the need for fancy equipment, massive teams, and distribution channels, it's easier to create and share our work with the world. With nothing more than a microphone and a laptop, a podcaster can record a show that reaches thousands of people. For example, in 2015, the comedian Marc Maron hosted President Obama in his studio—located in his garage—to interview him on his podcast *WTF*.

While you need certain skills to make it in a crowded lineup, you might be imagining lots of barriers, or a lack of skills, between you and the goal you're trying to accomplish, between you and catching waves. Hacking it in the lineup will more often than not require you to take matters into your own hands, embrace discomfort, accept the unknown, learn new skills, and push yourself to new limits.

Out of frustration and the inability to find a technical co-founder, Mattan Griffel taught himself the programming language Ruby on Rails. He then translated his experience into an online course called "How to Build Pinterest from Scratch in 30 Days." He was eventually accepted to the well-known start-up incubator Y Combinator, which led to the creation of his venture-funded accelerated learning start-up One Month.

A musician can rent a studio, record tracks, and distribute them to her fans via iTunes. When Dresden Dolls lead singer Amanda Palmer was fed up with the broken economics of the music industry, she turned to Kickstarter and raised more than a million dollars directly from her fans to record her next album.

But the price of all this opportunity is more competition than ever before. To hack it in the lineup, to be unmistakable, "your stuff better be that much more epic than the next guy," according to Breather CEO and writer Julien Smith. Because it's so easy to share your work, projects without longevity rarely cut through the noise created by all the media we're consuming, available at our fingertips on a daily basis.

Anyone can put their art on Instagram for a week. Anyone can write a blog for ninety days (which is the time frame when most people quit). Anyone can record ten episodes of a podcast. With longevity you start to build and earn the trust of an audience. If they know you'll be back tomorrow, the next day, and the next day, they're much more likely to stick around.

While work that's unmistakable is infused with your signature and your DNA, it isn't about just you, but about the impact it has on other people. Ultimately it's another person who recognizes your work as something nobody else could have done but you. Your odds of being unmistakable are much higher if you make an imprint on another's memory. With so many inputs competing for someone's attention, the ones people can consistently rely on to inspire them end up making an unmistakable mark. That takes time and commitment.

LONGEVITY

If we are going to achieve unmistakable mastery of any craft, our view must be long term. By the time the work of a true master reaches most of us, she's committed a huge amount of time to her craft—we should think of her as a ten-year overnight success. Ten years or ten thousand hours, which Malcolm Gladwell made famous in his book *Outliers,* appears to be the point when you start to achieve the highest levels of mastery.

We might cringe at the thought of committing so much time to any one thing. But time is our greatest competitive advantage. Time is the one resource we all have in equal amounts and it's the only one that can't be replenished. It's the most valuable resource at our disposal, yet squandering it on things that don't add any value to our lives is so normal to most of us that we're not even conscious of it.

To prioritize your time to become a master of your craft, you must become deliberate about how you spend it. The first step is awareness. Laura Vanderkam, author of *What the Most Successful People Do Before Breakfast,* recommends tracking exactly how you spend your time for an entire week. Keep a journal of your activities and how much time you spend on them. For an even more in-depth look at how you spend your time, download an app like ATracker or Timely.

This exercise turns out to be a wake-up call for every person who does it. Often we've lulled ourselves into a false sense of productivity. In a world that is driven by Facebook status updates, tweets, and endless amounts of articles on major news sites, it becomes very easy to confuse activity with accomplishment. If 80 percent of your time is spent consuming other people's tweets, articles on the Internet, and Facebook status updates, you're probably logging a lot of activity that's leading to very little accomplishment.

After a week of tracking my activity, I was shocked and embarrassed by how much time I spent browsing social media Web sites, playing video games, and watching Netflix. Your natural temptation might be like mine was—to massively overhaul my entire life in one fell swoop. Like crash diets, this is a recipe for disaster. The key is to start small. Be deliberate about how you will spend ten minutes of your day. A week later increase it to twenty, then to thirty, and eventually an hour.

One of the best ways for anyone starting out to make time for mastery of a craft is to adopt what author Cal Newport describes as a "rhythmic philosophy of deep work scheduling."

According to Newport, "This philosophy argues that the easiest way to consistently start deep work sessions is to transform them into a simple regular habit. The goal, in other words, is to generate a *rhythm* for this work that removes the need for you to invest energy in deciding if and when you're going to go deep."

I incorporated the rhythmic philosophy into my work by developing the habit of writing one thousand words a day. I started with smaller word counts, with a goal to write a little bit more each day. I made my goal to develop a habit, and then increase the quantity from there. As a result I got into a rhythm.

While it might sound completely nuts, many productivity experts also recommend scheduling every minute of your day on your calendar:

Schedule when you'll check e-mail.

Schedule when you'll waste time (seriously).

Schedule when you'll do your most substantive work.

It's not a coincidence that the greatest creators of our time abide by daily rituals—which is also the title of a book by Mason Currey about the creative habits of those creators. Once you become aware of how you're spending your time, you'll be amazed at how much of it you actually have at your disposal to develop better habits. And habits are the foundation of mastering just about every skill. Variety might be the spice of life when it comes to experience, but it's the kiss of death when it comes to creative habits.

When we use our time to direct our energy and effort to our craft, we approach the possibility of mastery.

In an episode of the *Off Camera with Sam Jones* podcast,

actor Matt Damon spoke about his own path to mastering the craft of acting. For Damon, whose body of work has included iconic films like *Good Will Hunting, Ocean's Eleven, The Martian,* and many others, the ride started at the age of thirteen. While still in high school, he traveled to New York for auditions and made the decision that he would do this for the rest of his life. He was chasing small waves and putting in a significant amount of water time. What motivated him and his writing partner and fellow actor Ben Affleck to write the movie *Good Will Hunting* was an attempt to create their own jobs, to find their own wave to ride. He recalled his thinking at the time to interviewer Sam Jones: "This is never going to happen for us if we sit around and wait for it." By the time the movie came out, Damon had been working at the craft of acting for more than eleven years. Since then, he's been involved in nearly every aspect of filmmaking, including directing, writing, and producing.

If we look at Matt Damon's story closely, we'll notice many of the essential characteristics of becoming an unmistakable master. The ten-year and ten-thousand-hour rules apply to his career. One year after the mastery mark, he hit his stride. He had an unwavering conviction and commitment to his craft. Throughout his career he's made a habit of pushing himself just beyond his current ability. In addition to taking on a wide variety of roles as an actor, he wrote the film that put him on the map. In a thirty-year career, Damon has appeared in more than fifty-nine feature films. The body of work represents the waves he's caught, while the length of his career parallels his time in the water.

Unmistakable work is a process of self-discovery. We start

our ride not knowing what it is that makes us unmistakable, and a thread reveals itself through the creation of a body of work. Dots connect, patterns emerge, and our unmistakable gift is revealed. Time is the critical ingredient required for this to take place, hence the role of longevity and commitment in the quest to become unmistakable.

Even though I started what is now the *Unmistakable Creative* podcast in 2010, I didn't truly become unmistakable until 2014. It took four years of showing up every single week, experimenting, iterating, failing, and wiping out before I learned how to ride waves consistently. Every small wave prepared me to ride a bigger one.

As of this writing more than six hundred episodes of the *Unmistakable Creative* podcast have been recorded; more than a million words have filled Moleskine notebooks, blogs, and books; and my commitment to the craft of interviewing people and storytelling now extends over half a decade and growing. And I still see myself as a student of what I do as opposed to a master.

In a world that moves at breakneck speeds and is littered with disposable tweets and status updates, our perception of longevity can get somewhat warped. We can delude ourselves into thinking one year is a long time. Y Combinator president Sam Altman said a founder should expect to spend ten years building a start-up, and having a long-term view will be a founder's greatest competitive advantage because so few people have one. If you want to become unmistakable and a master of your craft, you have to think about longevity and commit.

ARTISTS IN THE ECHO CHAMBER

In 2006, comedian Demetri Martin recorded a hilarious sketch about life coaching on *The Daily Show*. When Demetri Martin asks a life coach what she does, and she tells him, he responds that "a life coach is like having a really good friend who charges." After Demetri finds out the qualifications to become a life coach are access to the Internet, passing an online course, and the ability to fill out a form, he refines his definition to "a life coach is like having a really expensive friend with limited credentials and hands."

Later in the sketch a potential client visits a life coach, and by the end of her sessions she discovers her calling to be a life coach. While slapstick and amusing, *The Daily Show* was making a broader statement about the cultural echo chamber we contribute to.

According to Wikipedia, "In media, an **echo chamber** is a situation in which information, ideas, or beliefs are amplified or reinforced by transmission and repetition inside an 'enclosed' system, where different or competing views are censored, disallowed, or otherwise underrepresented."

When creators become part of the echo chamber, they simply parrot and mimic what already exists.

Every single day people who aspire to get their work out into the world bank on winning the Internet lottery after reading about the latest viral success story. They study what went viral and then convince themselves that if they do the same thing, they can be an overnight hit too. Instead they contribute only to a virtual echo chamber, perpetuating an unsustainable mimicry epidemic. Their work is certainly not unmistakable.

- *People see the Web site of a successful business coach or author and copy the branding and design to the letter.*

- *A podcaster makes a small fortune from his show, and the result is an onslaught of people who copy the format exactly, changing little more than the name.*

- *A YouTube video that goes viral makes someone "famous" overnight, opening the door to an entertainment career, and thousands of people create pale imitations of it in the hopes of being noticed.*

- *A start-up develops a product that gets written about in the press, is deemed the next unicorn (start-up lingo for a billion-dollar company in the making), and receives a mountain of venture capital, whereupon companies follow suit in an attempt to replicate its success.*

We seem to forget that in each of these equations one variable leads to a drastically different outcome: the person who created or started the project. And when we don't take this into consideration we deny the very essence of what makes each of us unmistakable: the fact that there has never been and never will be somebody with our exact genetic makeup, our unique talent, our experiences and perspective. To leave this out is to leave the soul out of our work. A nonnegotiable fact of unmistakable work is that you'll never create it playing by everyone else's rules, and a defining characteristic of an unmistakable brand is deliberate defiance of the status quo.

While learning from people who know more than you do is great, you have to understand the difference between emulation and inspiration. Our actions need to be informed by rather than defined by the people we look up to. Imitation is not the greatest form of flattery. Adaptation is.

In 2009, the job market was a disaster and the country was in a recession. On average, a thousand résumés were submitted for every one position, even for low-paying jobs. If you were going to get hired, you had to find a way to distinguish yourself from the sea of résumés HR departments were drowning in.

A designer and writer named Jamie Varon figured out a way to stand out, starting one of the first viral job search campaigns titled "Twitter Should Hire Me." The campaign led to national media attention, job offers from several companies, and eventually created so much demand for her work that she ended up starting her own company.

I noticed her campaign and thought it was brilliant, so I decided to start my own version: "100 Reasons You Should Hire Me." I used a logo generator to make mine look exactly like the Google logo and started a Web site on blogger.com. The reasons for somebody to hire me were nothing more than the bullet points on my résumé in blog form:

- *I have an MBA.*
- *I went to Berkeley.*
- *I'm organized and creative.*

I sent the campaign to the team at a career Web site called BrazenCareerist.com and they agreed to feature it. I knew the project was a failure when I couldn't come up with one hundred reasons why anybody should hire me, it hadn't led to any job prospects, and its poor execution was more of a hindrance to getting a job than a catalyst. Strangers on the Internet told me my campaign was terrible and that it didn't make a compelling case for why somebody should hire me—in fact perhaps the opposite. While it failed for numerous reasons, looking back I'd say the biggest one was that it wasn't unmistakable. I was in the echo chamber, so I saw something that worked well for the person with the original idea and tried to copy it but failed.

Photographer Brandon Stanton is known for his wildly popular photography project *Humans of New York*. The premise of the project is simple. He walks around New York City, asks people questions, and posts a caption along with the photo. As of this writing, the Facebook page for *Humans of New York* has more than 17 million fans, and the photos are shared upward of six thousand times each.

I started noticing other "Humans of" for lots of other cities on Facebook. Some of them have had a small degree of success riffing on Stanton's idea. But the only one that's unmistakable is *Humans of New York*. Every photograph he takes tells a story of everyday people who may never be covered by the local news. The photographic style, the captions, and the subjects are the by-product of Brandon's unique perspective, the details he notices, and the way he inspires strangers to open up and be vulnerable, which he somehow also captures in his photographs.

As a result of approaching more than ten thousand strangers on the street, Brandon has seen virtually every response he might get from a person. And with that he's developed a level of ease and comfort that causes people to open up. Because of that, every picture he shoots creates an unmistakable connection with his audience.

Only he can do what he does in the way that he does. Copycats who simply try to take photos and write clever captions have never achieved the same level of success. It's not something only they could do.

Christian Lander started the humor blog *Stuff White People Like,* which spawned hundreds of copycats. The only one that was unmistakable was Christian Lander's, because it was born out of his own spontaneity, creativity, and life experience. He wasn't looking at what other people were doing. Says Christian, "People can smell desperation. You have to create something that you like and you honestly cannot set out hoping for success— it's your first step to failure."

When you see the kind of success that leads to Internet fame, you give in to your temptation to mimic it: *If it worked for them, it will work for me.*

In the process of discovering what makes you unmistakable, you might consider what author Austin Kleon refers to as "stealing like an artist." At first you might mimic the style of an artist or the voice of a writer to try out their styles, to get to know and develop your own. But to effectively steal like an artist in a way that will make you unmistakable you must have a diversity of inputs and learn from the masters, while also adding your own signature. Take what you learn, incorporate what resonates with you, and make it your own. Thus, you don't end up parroting or mimicking; other people's work can serve as your land lesson. Eventually you have to jump in the water to uncover your own unmistakable gifts.

TOO INVESTED TO QUIT

The reality of hacking it in the lineup is that you have to show up early, show up often, and stay late. Learning how to surf is actually a pretty miserable experience. You don't know what you're doing. You're a nuisance to other surfers and you're constantly falling off your board and taking gallons of water up your nose. Setting off on your own unmistakable destiny can be just as tough. It's hard to believe that an activity that starts out like this can become so pleasurable that it can define a person's life. But after you catch one good wave, make one piece of unmistakable art, you'll be so hooked that you'll keep coming back. The best advice I ever got about surfing was from a guy in a bar in San Diego who told me to "go fifty times and then you'll be too invested to quit."

I have embraced the idea of getting too invested to quit—and you should too if you want to become unmistakable. At the end of every summer, Craigslist is littered with ads for blue foam surfboards being sold by people who realized how much harder it was to learn how to surf than they thought it would be. This lesson applies to just about anything that's worth doing. Amateurs sell their boards. Professionals learn to surf. Amateurs start lots of things. Professionals stick with a few passions for the long haul. Professionals get too invested to quit.

A creative project or business venture has a similar learning curve and struggle. You have to put in your time to earn the respect of the lineup. At the beginning you're not going to know what you're doing. Nobody will take your work seriously, you'll make tons of mistakes, and it's possible not a single person will see, hear, or experience your work. You might feel too discouraged to keep going and your efforts might seem fruitless, but remember you need to catch just that first good wave and you'll be hooked.

After more than six hundred interviews and countless conversations, I've learned that what separates the people who hack it in the lineup from the ones who don't is persistence, plain and simple. I've seen people with far more natural talent than I have fail because they couldn't or wouldn't keep coming back. But persistence without a strategy, without learning from your mistakes, without actively pursuing how to improve, is like being a mouse on a treadmill. In a post on his blog, venture capitalist Fred Wilson said, "If you listed the habits of successful people, tracking and measuring would be near the top of that list. I see it with people, companies, and teams that I work with. I see it in my own behavior." What you're measuring isn't as important as getting in the *habit* of measuring something that enables you to see whether or not you're making progress toward the end you have in mind. That way you learn from your mistakes, come up with new strategies, get off the treadmill, and start moving in the direction you want to go.

After I finished business school, with no job prospects on the horizon, and started close to half a dozen blogs that failed to get any traffic or reach an audience, I realized that I really had no idea what I was doing. I needed to learn from someone who had actually built a popular blog. That's when I stumbled on a course called "Blog Mastermind," created by an Australian blogger named Yaro Starak.

I asked my dad if he would lend me the five hundred dollars to take Yaro's course. So I guess you could say my dad was the first investor in the *Unmistakable Creative*. Because I was now on the hook for the five hundred dollars, and because my dad was involved, it created a greater sense of accountability.

I was too invested to quit.

After attending a school her father founded in Pakistan that the Taliban had begun attacking, Malala Yousafzai gave a speech in 2008 titled "How Dare the Taliban Take Away My Basic Right to Education?" Shortly afterward, she began anonymously blogging for the BBC about the Taliban's effort to restrict education and stop girls from going to school. As a result she started to receive death threats. But that didn't dissuade her from continuing to speak up. She was too invested to quit—at a level that most of us can't even fathom. The stakes were so high that the potential downside of her activism was death. In 2012, she was shot by the Taliban, and she used the opportunity to garner worldwide attention and speak out even more about the right of all women to an education. She went on to win the

Nobel Prize for her work in education activism. As BBC journalist Mishal Husain wrote, "The voice of the girl whom the Taliban tried to silence a year ago has been amplified beyond what anyone could have thought possible." That's the power of becoming too invested to quit.

MAKING THE COMPETITION IRRELEVANT

When our company wants to commission a provocative piece of art for our brand, we go to only one person: Mars Dorian. We don't shop around. We don't compare. We e-mail Mars and tell him what we need. Because he's unmistakable, his style is so distinctive that nobody can replicate it; he's made himself an indispensable part of our work. I couldn't tell you who his competitors are because we never need them.

When you're truly unmistakable, the competition becomes completely irrelevant. You're not the *best* option, you're the *only* option.

When you're the only option, people don't price shop, compare, or wait for what you're selling to go on sale. If you're the only option, people wait in line to buy your product or work with you, regardless of what it costs, or in some cases regardless of what you're selling.

On New Year's Eve 2015, I was introduced to Cards Against Humanity for the first time. I know what you're thinking: what planet have I been on for the past decade? With the tagline "a party game for horrible people," a snarky and irreverent FAQ on their Web site with the question "How do you play the game?" linking to a post titled "Here are the fucking rules," Cards Against Humanity created an insurgent brand. When Cards Against Humanity decided to sell boxes of shit—literally—for Black Friday, it was deliberate defiance at its best. They published their customers' complaint letters on their blog. Then in an effort to completely shatter what their customers would expect, they donated all of the proceeds to charity. And it generated millions of dollars in free publicity.

They didn't teach this in business schools or corporate training programs or include it as a lesson in business books. Combining irreverent marketing with acts of deliberate defiance, and clearly ignoring what conventional wisdom would say they "should" do, has made Cards Against Humanity an unmistakable brand.

In contrast, I have a scented candle on my desk. I have no idea who made it. I picked it out because of the way it smells and because it was cheaper than the other options. If somebody replaced it with another one that looked and smelled the same, I wouldn't notice. There's nothing unmistakable about it.

Intuit chairman Bill Campbell was known as the "CEO Whisperer" of Silicon Valley. He was brought in to coach CEOs of prominent start-ups and companies like Twitter and Apple. No one could go in his place because people wanted only him. He was unmistakable because nobody worked with the range of successful CEOs that he did—like Apple's Steve Jobs, Google's Larry Page, and Amazon's Jeff Bezos—and generated the kinds of results he did for his clients.

If you're the only option, nothing and no one can replace what you do. Any attempt at it would be a pale imitation that in the long run would fail to live up to expectations. If you're trying to be the best, you're still in a game of comparison and competition. You're abiding by the same rules and the same goals as everyone else around you—someone else's rules. While you might become the best, people still might not buy what you're selling or work with you. Perhaps it costs too much and they can find something that's almost as good for a little less. Playing the game of trying to be the best means there's always someone better or worse, and you're just stumbling over one another trying to beat them to the finish line. You might be in a race to the top, but the best you can do is simply better than your competition. Over a long enough time, this rat race leads to the commoditization of your work and ultimately a race to the bottom. If your product or service can be replicated, automated, and outsourced to the lowest bidder, you'll eventually be washed up in a sea of sameness.

If you choose to pursue the incredibly difficult work of becoming the *only,* however, your competition will eventually become irrelevant. You're not abiding by others' rules, therefore no one can compete with you, instead they can simply try to mimic you (and fail). But creating unmistakable work might be one of the hardest things to do: you have to look into the depths of who you are, explore what matters to you, and infuse that into every element of your work until it can't possibly be mistaken for something anybody could have done but you. You have to put in the extra effort even when you don't think you can give any more. You have to take pride in the parts of your craft that people will never see and probably wouldn't appreciate if they saw. You need the guts to destroy bad art. You have to become the benchmark, set the standard and obliterate that standard over and over again. What you create has to be so good, and have so much value, that it simply can't be ignored. You'll have to be deliberate about every ounce of work that you put out into the world, push boundaries, reinvent categories, defy people's expectations, and overwhelm them with joy. And it can't just be something you do in one blog post, one interaction, one work of art; it has to become your central ethos. In the TV show *Friday Night Lights,* coach Eric Taylor tells young quarterback Matt Saracen, "You need to know this offense in your mind, in your body. You need to know this offense so well that your children are going to know this offense in their own DNA." The same goes for unmistakable.

One of the hardest parts of unmistakable work is that no map, formula, or foolproof plan exists to get there. Online courses and books sell people on several-step methods and plans. But being able to follow a prewritten set of rules that lead to a predetermined outcome is not unmistakable. Very few of the wildly successful bloggers, podcasters, and YouTube stars have followed someone else's instructions to the letter. As designer Paul Jarvis once said, "Nobody is successful because they copied someone else's map." Either they ditched the map or they never had one to begin with.

BEST PRACTICES: YOUR WORST ENEMY

Those who choose to follow a map buy into the seductive promise of best practices. An individual or organization produces an outstanding result of some sort. They distill that result into a few key elements and package it up as a series of best practices, a how-to book, or a case study. MBAs, marketing managers, and other business professionals study these best practices in the hope that they might replicate some of the results.

Many of these so-called best practices would be more honest if the following disclaimer preceded them:

This is what we did. This is what happened. We've turned them into some principles. They might work for you. They might not.

Best practices and rules that people follow are inherited and thrust upon us. If we start to ask why things are done a certain way, threads start to unravel. What we often discover is that the only reason things are done a certain way is because they've always been done that way. In 1999 Shawn Fanning ignored all best practices when he created the music downloading application Napster. The music industry fought him and Napster, partly because it existed outside of best practices. The way things were always done is now the ghost we remember of what the music industry used to be, turning it into a cautionary tale. Tradition is a stupid reason to continue a best practice that produces suboptimal results.

In my personal experience at Pepperdine's MBA program, and looking at the course offerings of other business schools, they haven't updated curricula in decades even though they clearly need to do so. The traditional career path—get straight A's, go to college, and find a job—has been dismantled before our eyes, yet people are still doing it the same old way, which leads to mountains of student debt instead of pinnacles of success. Similarly, the eight-hour workday is a product of the Industrial Revolution and is still integrated into many organizations, though most people no longer even work in factories.

Best practices are a perfect cop-out. They let you off the hook. If what you tried doesn't work, then you can blame the system, the manual, or the author who wrote the book. When you take the risk to make something unmistakable, there's nobody to blame. You come up with the ideas and push boundaries, so you get all the credit when the work is incredible but all the blame when it falls short. But the price of playing it safe is that your work will become nothing more than a sad imitation of what's in the instruction manual, another case study to exemplify why everyone else in the future should follow this established best practice. In the words of cartoonist and author Hugh MacLeod, "The web has made kicking ass easier to achieve and mediocrity harder to sustain." By following best practices, we limit the potential outcomes of our work, increase the likelihood of mediocrity, and decrease the possibility of being unmistakable.

Designer and writer AJ Leon and his band of misfits broke all the rules of conferences. Instead of holding their Misfit conference in a big city or central hub, they get together in Fargo, North Dakota. Instead of choosing a lineup of giant keynote recognizable names, they invite speakers who are up to something fascinating and making a mark in the world. Instead of selling as many tickets as possible, they limit each conference to less than fifty attendees. These principles go against almost every best practice for planning a conference. The result is an unmistakable experience that people can't get enough of, and no alternative or anything you can compare it to. People go to Misfit because they want to have *that* experience.

I came face-to-face with best practices in the process of designing the *Unmistakable Creative* Web site. My mentor Greg Hartle and I started by asking who else had a really great "About" page, both for inspiration and to learn what we wanted. It wasn't until we shut down our laptops and ignored all the best practices for creating a company "About" page that our best ideas started to emerge. Our "About" page at Unmistak ableCreative.com includes cartoons—as you can imagine, no article we read about branding and "About" pages suggested this, but it fits our brand. If your company's "About" page is a summary with a series of headshots of executives (which is about 90 percent of companies), you might considering asking yourself, "How can we make it unlike any other 'About' page we've ever seen?" And to get started, shut down your laptop and let your imagination run riot.

By combining various art forms—the violin, choreography, and film—and ignoring best practices, Lindsey Stirling has redefined the standards of what's possible in the career of a violinist. Juilliard is probably not teaching Lindsey Stirling's approach to art in its classrooms, but more than 100 million people have watched several of her videos on YouTube—and her art is certainly unmistakable. As a result of combining all three art forms, she has made her competition irrelevant.

In business, Basecamp cofounders David Heinemeier Hansson and Jason Fried broke nearly every rule of building a successful software company. Ironically, they rewrote the best practices by breaking the rules. They write one-page proposals instead of ten-page business plans. Their team is scattered across the world rather than working nine-to-five in one office together. Meetings are seen as toxic to their culture. The result is a successful organization that has made millions of dollars and created millions in value for their customers.

In religion, megapastor Rob Bell found himself bored to tears at church when he first started out. Before he became a pastor, Rob was in a band. "You don't stand through a band that isn't engaging you," explained Rob in an interview on the *Unmistakable Creative*. "Everybody was there because they wanted to see a show that would make them say to their friends, 'You missed a great one.' Why would you go do something just because you're supposed to?" The lesson of engaging an audience was not lost on Rob when he became a pastor: "The idea that you would go to church because you were supposed to just blew my mind. When I started preaching, for me the sermon was like this art form, like guerrilla theater, like performance art."

By creating a community with room for doubt, discovery, and disbelief, and discussing the most important questions about what it means to live a meaningful life in a fascinating, provocative way, Rob has completely changed the experience of church. Instead of dread and checking out during service, congregants look forward to Sundays and actively participate.

Similarly, when graffiti artist and author Erik Wahl became a keynote speaker, he didn't go to Toastmasters or study other keynote speakers. In an effort to understand how to electrify a twenty-first-century audience, Erik studied live music, comedy, and other art forms outside of his industry rather than follow best practices. As a result, he mixes live painting, music, and a motivational speech that keeps his audience completely involved. "Live music engages participants," says Wahl. "Keynote speaking has passive consumers. There's room to be explored in how you bridge that gap." For Wahl, the competition is completely irrelevant because no other corporate keynote speaker does what he does.

While you might be thinking, "Great, now that best practices and studying the best of my industry are thrown out the window, how am I supposed to know what to do?" All of these examples show that these inspiring creatives took a very different approach from everyone else to arrive at unmistakable. This book is here to help you break down all the rules that you think you must abide by, all the goals you think you need to be part of the rat race to achieve faster than someone else, and to help you exit the echo chamber so you can be the only you. You can achieve unmistakable work by charting your own course and following what inspires you.

If you look closely at the examples above, certain patterns start to emerge—a consistent theme of ignoring or altogether defying expectations of what many of these things should look like:

- *We don't expect violinists to mix in dubstep dancing and provocative music videos. We typically expect them to be playing concertos in concert venues where symphony orchestras perform.*

- *We don't expect conferences to be held in small towns with a lineup of speakers that are largely unknown. We typically expect them to be held in big cities, in hotel ballrooms with household names as speakers.*

- *We don't expect the experience of going to church to be comparable to guerrilla theater or a rock concert. We expect it to be long, monotonous, and something we endure to increase our chances of getting into heaven.*

- *Unless you're a professional cartoonist, your Web site won't have cartoons on the "About" page for a company because it's not good for search engine optimization (SEO). We typically expect to find a company description, followed by headshots of the executive team and summaries of their biographies.*

By ignoring best practices, deliberately defying expectations, and creating what each individual and organization inwardly felt deeply compelled to create and wanted to see exist in the world, these creatives' work became unmistakable and their competition got left behind, scrambling to figure out how to change course to copy a new best practice disrupting the industry.

If you need some guidance and want to use best practices to become unmistakable, don't look at what your own industry is promoting as what's best. Look at other art forms that have mastered the ability to overwhelm people with joy for inspiration. While the world is filled with business books that are chock-full of great advice, a question worth asking yourself is whether you should follow anyone's advice to the letter. I don't believe authors write business books in the hopes that people will treat their work like a connect-the-dots how-to manual, like a map. I certainly don't want you to do that with this book. What I hope is that you treat it like a compass.

THE GREATEST WORK OF YOUR LIFE WILL REQUIRE A COMPASS, NOT A MAP

When you're impossible to replicate, you've started to trust your inner compass. Unmistakable work is a combination of unpredictable and delightful. A surfer's compass opens up the entire planet to travel, and the pursuit of waves is a lifetime adventure that leads us to places we'll never find on any map.

Trusting and using your inner compass as a guide can be learned, but it can't be taught. Once I ditched my map, all I had was a surfboard, a compass, and a life filled with uncertainty. Where the compass would point me was an unknown, but what unfolded on the way were experiences, unexplored shores, and perfect waves yet to be surfed that I could only have gotten to if I was willing to meander without a map.

For over a decade I used a map with clearly marked destinations:

- *College at Berkeley*
- *An MBA*
- *A well-paying, cushy job in Silicon Valley*

But the landscape changed so drastically that following that map led to a dead end. I didn't find a cushy job waiting for me at the end of my MBA, and to top it off, I'd attempted to sell off pieces of my soul to the highest bidder (i.e., potential employers). That's when I realized it was time to ditch the map and script for a surfboard, a wetsuit, and a compass.

You probably prefer using a map because it's more comfortable and less anxiety producing. But the problem is that you know where you're going, where you'll end up, and what roads lead there. While that's not a terrible result—similar to trying to be the best—unmistakable work instead requires that you abandon the map somewhere along the way and open yourself up to destinations and ideas that you can't predict or plan for.

I had only one goal when I wrote my first blog: get a day job. Needless to say the ship sailed far off course. The *Unmistakable Creative* podcast largely exists because I ditched my map for a compass. One of the lessons in an online course I took was "conduct one interview with someone as a way to get traffic to your blog." No part of that lesson included turning the interview into a weekly series, then a separate Web site, and next a podcast show that is still running five years later. I deviated from the lesson plan and it made all the difference.

Going off course and using my compass has led to other unmistakable work. I've produced an animated series with Soul-Pancake (which made the viral Kid President videos) that premiered on a YouTube channel with 1.5 million subscribers. I've had conversations with some of the most unmistakably interesting people on the planet, from cartoonists, tech entrepreneurs, ex-cons, and psychologists to people with unusual projects like walking a dog across America. I've launched an online art store to sell T-shirts, posters, and other cool merchandise. I've written more than one million words. I've made friends from all over the world, and my work has added more meaning to my life than I could ever have imagined was possible.

None of those activities were clearly marked destinations on a map. They were the result of going where the compass pointed me. When you ditch your map for a compass, you evolve dramatically as a person. Because you don't know exactly where you're headed, limits and borders in your life and work cease to exist. While terrifying at first, this process is liberating once you start to see what it can do for you and where you can go as a result. When you treat people's advice as a map, the best you can do is end up exactly where they did. But if you're going to become unmistakable, you have to learn to use a compass.

Letting go of your need for a map isn't easy because you have to break a lifetime of conditioning. Tina Seelig is a director of the Stanford Technology Ventures Program and a professor at Stanford's design school. Some of her young students have their entire lives mapped out in precise detail. Tina likes to ask these students, "Where's the room for serendipity in that?" If you're eighteen and reading this book, I feel compelled to tell you that life is probably not going to go according to your perfectly mapped-out plan. Don't worry, that's a good thing; hard, but good.

In school and perhaps in the working world you've been rewarded by following instructions perfectly. In any creative or entrepreneurial endeavor you'll be rewarded for realizing that all instructions, all rules, and all best practices are open to interpretation. Tina Seelig says, "Most rules are just recommendations."

Author and designer Colin Wright literally travels without a map. Every three months he allows the readers of his blog, ExileLifestyle.com, to vote where he should move to next. He does no research on his new home and lets the adventure unfold. The result is countless conversations and unmistakable stories that would never occur if he used a map.

Clara Bensen took losing her map to a whole other level when meeting a guy on OkCupid led to traveling with him across the world with no reservations, either logistical or emotional: "Traveling with no luggage and no plans," Bensen writes in her *Salon* article "The Craziest OkCupid Date Ever," "was much more than a minimalist lesson in living well with less. It was an intense, in-your-face invitation to the unknown. There's a truly magnificent side to the unknown, but we aren't taught how to welcome it, let alone explore the breadth of its possibilities."

A compass welcomes the unknown and the breadth of possibilities that come with it. Ditch the map, grab a surfboard, and let the compass guide you unmistakably.

Unmistakable Creative: Golriz Lucina

Chief creative officer and executive producer Golriz Lucina is the coauthor of SoulPancake: Chew on Life's Big Questions. *Founded by actor Rainn Wilson, SoulPancake is an award-winning media company that is known for creating meaningful entertainment that explores the human experience and engages a socially minded, global audience. SoulPancake's YouTube video "Kid President" has more than 38 million views to date, and the Oprah channel has commissioned a series.*

When Golriz's husband Devon Gundry teamed up with actor Rainn Wilson to create SoulPancake, the team took the risk to pursue an uncertain path with no stability, no revenue models, and no guaranteed paycheck. Which is the pursuit of unmistakable work—it doesn't come with any guarantees. Instead of following old formulas to replicate her previous success, her intuition and instinct drive the creative process of her work at SoulPancake. Her willingness to create work that's meaningful as opposed to manufactured, that touches hearts instead of attempting to maximize eyeballs or clicks, continually makes her work unmistakable.

Start with What You Love

While most people follow the rules and then realize what they love, Golriz instead began by asking, "What do I love? Let's start from there." The voyage to her role as chief creative officer started with a master's degree in publishing and editing. After a stint as an editor, she found herself in Nashville, Tennessee, working as a marketer for touring Broadway shows. Shortly after, she met her husband Devon, and with Rainn Wilson, they began SoulPancake. The Web site was based on the fact that they "didn't have the answers. We just wanted to create a place for people to explore. We wanted to have deeper, richer conversations with each other, and we were pleasantly surprised to find we weren't the only ones."

To arrive at our own version of unmistakable, we might have a lot of different, seemingly unrelated stops along the way. We might work jobs that seem like they have nothing to do with the future we're planning for. We might unexpectedly end up in parts of the world or our country we had never planned to. But it's within the unexpected, almost random patterns that innovation, creativity, and unmistakable ideas often begin to take form. "Looking back now," said Golriz, "it makes so much sense. Every one of those little decisions led me to here."

Intuition and Instinct

Golriz's creative process reaffirms that really no formula exists for creating unmistakable work.

We'll get calls from people who want something that feels like this X piece that we made. I can't tell them, "Okay, the formula is get a charismatic kid from Tennessee, add two parts of an amazing script, and then throw in some incredible music and some good color, and boom! There you have it, a viral video that's going to affect hearts and minds." Unfortunately it isn't that tactical. It is intuition and instinct.

Rather than asking herself how she can replicate something that went viral, the question Golriz uses to shape the content for SoulPancake is "How can I use this as a conduit for unity?"

When we've experienced success in any capacity, it might be tempting to extrapolate a formula to repeat that success. But when we neglect intuition and instinct, our work suffers. If we start with the more challenging question of how we might affect hearts and minds, the likelihood of creating something unmistakable goes up.

How Limited Resources Fuel Creativity

SoulPancake's earliest content reflected having to work with limited resources. Because the initial work wasn't slick, scripted, and polished, "people resonated with the fact that it felt like someone's hand had made this, that someone had poured a lot of love and heart into this," Golriz recounts.

In fact, her belief that "time limits or money limits force you to focus and create the best with what you've got" informed the wedding she planned with her then-fiancé:

> We got really zany about it all and that's what made it so memorable and such a sweet experience that was flooded with us. We didn't have the money for the most expensive flowers or the most expensive food, yet we pulled off the wedding of my dreams.

If we let them, limited resources can become a form of resistance, procrastination, and an excuse to avoid working. On the other hand, limited resources can result in more creative, heartfelt, and emotionally resonant work, as they did for Golriz and the SoulPancake team. Rather than seeing our resources as limited, if we start with the question "What can we do with what we've got?," the set of possible solutions to any problem we're trying to solve immediately expands.

Defining Unmistakable

Golriz defines unmistakable this way: "When something is coming from authenticity, when you're creating from your own blueprint, when it's genuine and sincere and true, that's what makes something unmistakable."

PART 3:

There's a moment just after a surfer paddles for a wave—when he angles the board parallel to the direction that the wave will go, pushes himself up, and stands up on the board—when everything is at stake. That liminal moment between paddling and standing is known as the drop, and even though the drop is brief, it determines what your entire ride will be like. In the context of business or art, the way you approach the drop will determine whether or not you manage to get your work out into the world, achieve your goals, and have your intended impact.

On some waves the drop might be soft and forgiving, and the margin for error is a bit higher. But on the most difficult, biggest, and rewarding waves, the drop is incredibly steep. The wave looks like a mountain made of water, and your heart races in anticipation of an amazing ride or a horrific wipeout. It takes nerves of steel to stare down the face of that kind of wave and believe that you will actually make it. You have to have what Google cofounder Larry Page calls "a healthy disregard for the impossible."

The drop is that moment when you go all in, when there's no turning back. When you walk out the door of a safe and secure job with a guaranteed paycheck to pursue a calling, you're in the drop. When you've committed to delivering a product or experience to someone who has paid you for your work, you're in the drop. When you've signed a contract with a venue for an event, and the deposit is nonrefundable, you're in the drop.

The drop is the point of no return.

The drop is a perfect metaphor for the commitment required to create unmistakable work. The beginning of a creative or entrepreneurial endeavor is a major turning point in your life. The more committed you are, the more likely you are to experience success. If you hesitate on the drop, the ride will be messy, you'll be struggling to stay on your board, and the possibility of a wipeout increases significantly. When surfers hesitate on the drop, they start to lose the respect of the lineup and aren't taken seriously. If you charge the drop with everything you have, fully committed, your odds of an unmistakable ride go up drastically.

Every single thing you create or start is like a wave, and the drop is a moment that you will arrive at over and over again in your quest to become unmistakable.

THE STEEPER THE DROP, THE GREATER THE REWARD

Laird Hamilton is a big-wave surfer who exemplifies doing the impossible. From looking at him, you would think he's either blessed with incredible genes or spends all his time in the gym. He appears to be pure muscle, and at the age of fifty-two he's in better physical shape than most people are in their twenties. All of this is because of an insane commitment to diet and being the ultimate waterman. Name a water sport in the ocean—stand-up paddleboarding, surfing, bodyboarding, swimming—Laird has done it. I came across a YouTube video of him and have never experienced quite such a visceral understanding as when I saw him drop into a seventy-foot wave.

Hamilton is not necessarily fearless, but he sees fear in a different way from most people. He sees it as something that gives him power. In *Outside* magazine, he said, "Fear is an unbelievable motivator, but it also makes people freeze in their tracks. Once you understand it, fear becomes something you can tap into. Fear comes from the understanding that you can die. It usually makes me make really good decisions and gives me power."

Laird perceives possibility on the other side of his fear, so he's continually redefining the limits of big-wave surfing in an unmistakable way. He sets a standard by which many big-wave surfers are judged.

When you charge a wave, the consequences of a wipeout could be dire. You could be held underwater for up to four minutes (something big-wave surfers have to learn as part of their training) as you take wave after wave on the head, wondering if you'll ever come up for air. You might get tossed around like you're inside a saltwater washing machine as what feels like gallons of water go up your nose. Or the board might smack you upside the head causing your eardrum to burst (ironically, that happened to me on the smallest of waves). Your fears are not unjustified.

But what if you could see fear as a sign of the greatness that's on the other side, like Laird Hamilton? Often our fear is a signal that what's on the other side is bliss, and miracles start to occur only when we attempt to do those things that scare us. What if you could see fear as a sign that you're standing on the edge of something daring, something that could truly change your life? What if on the other side of fear is an opportunity to overcome limitations you think you have, and discover abilities you thought you didn't? When you're surfing, staring down the face of a wave with a really steep drop, what helps you not to hesitate is knowing that the ride can be incredible.

With each wave you catch, you start to shed layers of fear, doubt, and uncertainty that have kept you from being unmistakable. Every wave is a test of your commitment. The more ambitious your dream is, the steeper the drop will be. To make the drop, you have to be able to see the future, the possibility of a wave that will open up for you and lead to the ride of your life.

I wish I could tell you exactly how much time creating unmistakable work is going to take. But I can't. I've been producing content on the Internet since 2009. My first big break was in 2014 when I self-published *The Art of Being Unmistakable*. I made a five-year commitment before I experienced any major external markers of success. That's a really steep drop.

What I do know is that if you're serious, it will most likely take longer than you want. If you aren't willing to commit at least a year of your life to doing work every single day, charging your wave with everything you have, you should stop reading this book right now. You have to put in a lot of water time to learn how to commit on the drop. If you're up for it, keep reading.

About Time and Timing

Every now and then friends of mine will tell me that they want to learn to surf. They ask me if I'll take them out. Before I agree, I always warn them that they will need to show up for several days in a row. The pattern I've consistently noticed with the people who never figure out how to stand up is that they never come back the next day. They're not committed.

I have other friends who are notorious for bouts of inspiration that happen once every six months on a Saturday afternoon when mindless social media check-ins, Netflix binges, and other distractions aren't able to keep their attention. So they research, plan, and even take a few steps toward their business idea or artistic project. The way they start is the clearest indication that they'll never finish, that they're going to hesitate on the drop. If the Saturday afternoon doesn't lead to overnight fame and riches, they don't bother again for another six months. It's like getting in the water every few months and wondering why you're having such a difficult time catching waves. The Internet is littered with the digital graveyards of people who have spent one random afternoon a year trying to make their mark on the world.

In their book *The Impact Equation,* Julien Smith and Chris Brogan talk about frequency as one of the essential variables required to make an impact:

> *Exposure is the art of hitting people, again and again until they finally decide to take some kind of action. At its simplest,*

exposure is frequency. It's what makes the prospective car buyer finally walk into the Nissan dealership or what happens when the blogger is finally able to convince readers to give him their e-mail address. It's what happens when the New York Times *finally gets someone to agree that yes, perhaps its offering is worth paying premium prices for.*

Your posture in the drop is a decision about how much you're willing to give to the wave you're going for. What are you willing to commit? Time, energy, and money? And how much of it are you willing to commit? You need to commit a lot of at least one, if not each.

Jon Acuff, author of books such as *Quitter* and *Do Over,* articulates how we expect to be good at things way too quickly after we've started. We spend ten years as an accountant and one year as an artist, but complain we're not as accomplished an artist as we are an accountant.

The story of Pixar is exemplary of how logging an insane amount of time in the water and committing to an incredibly steep drop can lead to catching some really big waves. Ed Catmull, John Lasseter, and Steve Jobs, the founding team at Pixar, were ahead of their time. The demand for their Pixar Image Computers wasn't very high, and the idea of a feature-length computer-animated film was unheard of. In his book about Pixar, *Creativity, Inc.,* Catmull writes:

Why were we so deep in the red? Because our initial flurry of sales died away almost instantly—only three hundred Pixar

Image Computers were ever sold—and we weren't big enough to design new products quickly. We had grown to more than seventy people, and our overhead was threatening to consume us. As the losses mounted, it became clear that there was only one path forward: We needed to abandon selling hardware. . . . The only thing that made this leap easier was that we had decided to go all in on what we'd yearned to do from the outset: computer animation.

Many times Pixar was on the verge of running out of money. They almost ceased to exist.

Nearly twenty years and millions of dollars later, they finally caught the big wave of producing feature-length computer-animated films. But when they made the decision to abandon selling computer hardware and go all in on computer animation, they committed to a really steep drop and the possibility of riding a massive wave. What's followed has been blockbusters like *Toy Story, The Incredibles, Monsters, Inc., Inside Out, Finding Nemo,* and many others. And that's because they stayed in the water and remained committed to their vision.

Unmistakable work requires you to be committed to what you're yearning to do from the outset, even if things don't go exactly as planned along the way.

At the Podcast Movement 2015, an annual conference held in Dallas, one of the keynote speakers was comedian and podcaster Marc Maron. In 2009 when Maron started his podcast *WTF,* how it would work was a complete unknown. His comedy career had gone up in flames, his wife had left him, and he said his podcast was "an alternative to suicide." Maron committed to a steep drop. He wrestled with questions like how the show would find an audience and be funded.

One wave at a time, Maron started to rebuild his career. He started selling T-shirts to pay for the show. As the show grew, more and more high-profile comics like Robin Williams and Louis C.K. started to make appearances. As the caliber of the guests increased, the show grew in popularity.

Today *WTF with Marc Maron* reaches millions of listeners, and guests have included well-known actors, artists, and even the president of the United States. Maron's comedy career has been revitalized thanks to his own television show and having an outlet to let millions of fans know about his upcoming performances.

Our natural tendency when the unexpected occurs is to imagine the worst-case scenarios. But a willingness to put ourselves at risk and face the unknown opens us up to possibility. When we know how everything will turn out, our outcomes are certain, guaranteed, and predictable, and we're blinded to other possibilities that, while unpredictable, could be far more rewarding. Uncertainty and the unknown, while seemingly terrifying, are what enable us to create drastic changes in our lives the way Maron did. As my friend Reema Zaman says, "Uncertainty is a form of limitlessness." So if you're standing on the edge of uncertainty, write down a list of all the possibilities that may come from pursuing this route instead. You might find yourself staring down the drop of a really big wave that will lead to a hell of a ride, as Kimberly Bryant did.

Since she founded her organization Black Girls Code in 2011, Kimberly Bryant's work has resulted in a movement for girls to learn to code and be introduced to technology and programming from a young age. Starting with only twelve students in Bayview–Hunters Point, one of San Francisco's poorest neighborhoods, her organization has expanded to chapters in at least seven cities across the United States as of this writing, and an international chapter in Johannesburg, South Africa. Black Girls Code has grown to include more than two thousand girls and counting.

With a goal to have a million girls coding by the year 2040, Kimberly Bryant has committed to an incredibly steep drop, one that will be the work of a lifetime.

What Ed Catmull, Marc Maron, and Kimberly Bryant have in common is a long-term dogged commitment to working toward their goals and making them a reality.

Risk

Every time I paddle for a wave, I take a risk. I know that I might not make it. When a wave closes out, it appears to be rideable, but like having a rug pulled out from under you, the entire wave unexpectedly crumbles, leaving a surfer nowhere to go but down for a wipeout. The bigger the wave you attempt to ride, the greater the risk, the deeper the commitment required. The rewards are proportionate to the risks you take.

No unmistakable achievement occurs without the willingness to take a risk. It's one of the critical ingredients. Just as you put your heart on the line for love, you need to do the same to be unmistakable.

Jonathan Fields explains risk and what you stand to lose—and gain—by taking one in his book *Uncertainty*:

> *Whenever you set out to do what's never been before or never been done in the way you want to do it, you risk losing all sorts of things, time that could have been spent on something else, money that could have been saved, prestige, status, income or the perception of security. But the possibility of loss is also a signpost that what you're doing really matters, that you're vested in both the process and the outcome. Knowing that fuels a deeper commitment to action and to striving not just to create something, but to create something amazing.*
>
> *Risk of loss has to be there. You cannot create genius without having skin in the game. Kill the risk of loss and you destroy the meaning and one of the core motivations for action.*

Entrepreneurial and creative endeavors perfectly parallel the risk in the drop.

It's possible that people will hate the product you're inventing.

It's possible that nobody will buy the art that you're selling.

It's possible that you'll lose time, energy, and money in the process.

It's a balance of embracing the possibility of failure while trusting that you will succeed. The fastest path to believing that you will succeed is by making what author Peter Sims refers to as "little bets," low-risk ideas that give you enough feedback and confidence to evolve and grow.

Sims explains in his book *Little Bets,* "If we haven't invested much in developing an idea, emotionally or in terms of time or resources, then we are more likely to be able to focus on what we can learn from that effort than on what we've lost in making it." Little bets are instrumental to the creative process and help reduce some of the anxiety and fear in taking the giant plunge of risking it all toward unmistakable.

By the time a comedian like Chris Rock takes the main stage in a huge venue on a tour, all of his material has been tested at open mic nights at local comedy clubs. Those local appearances are Rock's little bets. As a result he has the confidence to know that people will laugh when he performs his act in front of thousands of people.

Little bets have been a fundamental part of my process at the *Unmistakable Creative.* My self-published book *The Art of Being Unmistakable* was nothing more than a PowerPoint presentation based on a talk I had given at AJ Leon's Misfit conference. The same way Chris Rock tests his stand-up material, I used a live audience to test everything I'd written for resonance. Even some of the material you're reading in this book, a sentence here, an occasional Facebook status update, or a tweet, have all been tested.

In my first year of surfing, I would read the surf report

hoping that the waves weren't too big. As my skills evolved, I gradually worked my way up to surfing bigger waves. With every bigger wave I surfed, the boundaries of my comfort zone changed. Every small wave prepared me for the bigger ones.

I see now how the size of the waves I've gone for as I've progressed and the level of ambition in all my creative and entrepreneurial endeavors tie together. Small projects give us the confidence and daring to try something bigger, to double down on the little bet we've made and continue toward unmistakable.

It took me a year to gather the courage to publish an e-book and ask people to pay for it. The book was riddled with typos. But I had finally stepped up and gone for a bigger wave.

I also went for a lot of waves that I didn't manage to catch or completely wiped out on. We launched a membership portal for our podcast listeners that didn't generate enough revenue to justify continuing it. I self-published a book called *Blog to Book Deal: How They Did It,* which was nothing more than transcripts of our interviews. It didn't sell, wasn't particularly well written or curated, and above all, it failed because I did it for the wrong reasons, not to provide value or make something I was proud of. I was hoping to cash in on all the aspiring bloggers who had dreams of getting a book deal. My intention wasn't pure and that came through in the quality of the work.

But in 2013, I started to charge waves like I never had before. My primary motive was no longer fame, success, and accolades, but impact and significance. I was driven by longing for my work to matter, be meaningful, and touch people's hearts.

I'm not sure what caused it. Perhaps it was the front-row

seat I had to seeing my parents age. Maybe it was looking in the mirror and noticing that I didn't look the same as I did even two years ago. I had more gray hair than I'd seen before.

The notion that life is short, that we should live it to the fullest and dance like nobody's watching makes for nice motivational posters, Instagram memes, and Hallmark greeting cards. But the conversations I was having with people on the podcast transformed all these platitudes into one unquestionable truth: we're all going to die. Maybe not tomorrow, maybe not next year, maybe not even in twenty years. As I came to understand that truth, it left me with one question, which I'd encourage you to ask yourself:

Have I created the most audacious and ambitious pieces of art and started the most daring projects that I want to see exist in the world?

With a resounding no as an answer, I felt a sense of urgency. I was done waiting for permission, waiting until I had enough authority, waiting until the audience who read my writing and listened to my podcast was bigger. I had to say everything that I was longing to say, build whatever I was longing to build, give the world whatever gifts I felt compelled to leave it before I was gone. And with that also came a desire to be more deliberate, to create beautiful unmistakable art, art that couldn't possibly be ignored.

It didn't matter whether the waves were big or small. I wrote a thousand words each day like my life depended on it. I published multiple pieces in addition to the interviews that we have published every Monday and Wednesday since the show started. I self-published two books: *The Small Army Strategy* and *The Art of Being Unmistakable*.

The biggest wave of my life so far was my first conference, the Instigator Experience. Before committing to booking a venue, I built a simple Web site asking people to enter their e-mail address if they were interested in attending the event. Every speaker had been a guest on the *Unmistakable Creative* podcast. Their messages had really struck a chord with our listeners. Every interview was a little bet. By the time we opened up applications for the event, more than six hundred people were on our e-mail list.

I went from charging three dollars for a book I had written to asking people to spend $1,300, commit two days, and fly across the country. My risks included:

- *Having invested six months into a project that might fall flat on its face—publicly.*

- *Letting down all the friends and former guests of the show I had asked to speak at the event. They had to plan their schedules almost nine months in advance and turn down other opportunities.*

- *Taking on the financial risk of signing a contract for a venue and being on the hook for the money whether the event took place or not.*

It scared the hell out of me, but ultimately paid off with an unforgettable event, in which I got to blend my love of art, movies, music, and theater into an unmistakable experience. But I couldn't have gotten there without all the small waves. It's tempting to overlook all the small things that go into a significant accomplishment because by the time it's on our radar, it appears to be larger than life. But if you take a closer look you'll see hundreds of iterations, small risks leading to bigger ones, and what appear to be massive risks. Every small wave prepares you for a bigger one and increases your tolerance for risk. The more waves you go for, the more you'll catch, and the bigger the waves you'll be able to ride.

Unmistakable Big-Wave Surfers

A few years ago, Jayson Gaignard ran a successful concert promotion business. Despite earning twenty-two times the national average income, he had passed the point where the money was enough and the endeavor no longer fed his soul.

Meanwhile, as part of the book launch for *The 4-Hour Body,* Tim Ferriss had offered to give a keynote talk—if someone bought $84,000 worth of his books. Jayson took Tim up on it without any idea how he would pay for it. But he was now on the hook for the money. He'd committed to a steep drop—there was no backing out.

Up until that point Jayson had been holding a series of Mastermind dinners, which he had started in 2012. The premise of the dinners was to invite a small group of entrepreneurs handpicked from his personal network to a monthly event.

But the risk of agreeing to spend $84,000 forced him to change his posture and get ready to ride a *much* bigger wave. By leveraging the fact that Tim Ferriss, a highly sought-after keynote speaker with limited availability, was on the roster, Jayson persuaded many other speakers to attend and speak for free and created a successful, invitation-only event called Mastermind Talks.

The cost to attend is more than $9,000 a person, but attendees have significant accomplishments: they have published books, built successful companies across numerous industries, and started social enterprises. A reporter for *Entrepreneur* magazine called Jayson and the event "One-man TED Talks."

Another big-wave surfer is Misfit AJ Leon, who left his high-profile investment banking job four days before his wedding. Not only that, he left a significant promotion on the table. As he describes in this excerpt from his collection of essays *The Life and Times of a Remarkable Misfit:*

> I used to be an unremarkably average finance executive in Manhattan. I made six figures, had an outrageous bonus and a corner office. But there was this little problem. I despised my job. I was passionless about my work. And of course, I hated myself for trading the hours of my life away for more money at every turn. On December 31, 2007, I left my six figures, crazy bonus, Manhattan corner office job. Not for a raise. Not in a vertical move to another company. Not to get a change of scene. But to stop, once and for all, living some other dude's life. That day I realized two things. There was more to life than working a job you hate, and more importantly, there was more to me than could ever be expressed in a place with so many rules.

So yeah, you might be thinking, of course he could leave if he was an investment banker with a six-figure salary. AJ had been spending money and budgeting for his wedding based on an investment banker's salary, however, so he and his wife, Melissa, didn't have a large nest egg to fall back on. But he took the risk anyway. Walking away from the job four days before his wedding was AJ's commitment to a steep drop with an unknown outcome.

AJ and Melissa used their frequent flier miles to hop on a flight to Africa to help kids in the developing world get on the Web. They had ninety-four Twitter followers and about $134 in the bank at the time. The first few weeks involved sleeping in airports, designing Web sites in exchange for room and board, and surviving off free potato chips. By the time you're reading this, it will have been close to nine years since AJ left his job. Today his and his wife's adventures have included traveling to fifty-five countries, building beautiful Web sites for products and companies they care about, raising millions of dollars for various nonprofits, and working with an incredible team of artists around the world.

With a For Dummies guide on how to sell on eBay, Sophia Amoruso started selling vintage clothing online. In the early days of the business she scoured thrift stores, auctions, and Craigslist for inventory. And she photographed friends to model the clothing. At the height of her success, Sophia risked leaving eBay to start her own site, unable to take any of her customer information and loyal fans with her. To launch and build Nasty Gal, it took, in her own words, "years of living with dirty fingernails from digging through vintage, a few painful burns from steaming clothes, and many an aged Kleenex in a coat pocket to get here." With her *New York Times* best-selling *#GIRLBOSS* book and Nasty Gal now a $250 million fashion line, Sophia Amoruso defines the big-wave surfer.

Jayson, AJ, and Sophia have fulfilled their ambitions because they took risks and committed to big waves with steep drops. We receive rewards in proportion to the risks we're willing to take and the sacrifices we're willing to make. The bigger the waves you're willing to go for, the crazier your ride will be.

Fear

When I ask listeners of the *Unmistakable Creative* podcast what keeps them from reaching their goals, they've all responded with some variation of fear:

- *Fear that nobody will read their work*
- *Fear that nobody will buy their products*
- *Fear that they'll completely fail*

Instead of charging the drop with everything they've got, these listeners had become almost paralyzed in the drop.

The drop is an amplifier of fear, and for the most part we try to avoid fear. But if we're going to ride the biggest and fastest waves, daring unmistakable work, we have to learn to embrace moments that amplify our fear.

You have to learn to charge the drop with everything you

have, to build it as a habit. And the only way to learn it is by doing it. The more you do it, the more likely you are to do it on every single wave that's yours for the taking. If you start with something small where the consequences of failure are real but not too high, you will start to build a muscle.

- *Write down a story that you've been afraid to share with the world, and publish it on a Web site like Medium.*

- *Record a video of yourself dancing like nobody's watching. Then upload it to YouTube and share it with some friends.*

- *Write a really vulnerable letter to someone close to you like a spouse, parent, or best friend.*

As you do these small things, you'll start to develop your capacity to charge the drop with everything you have.

We buy into this idea that someday fear will be gone and we'll be able to make the drop then. But it turns out that the opposite is true. When we make the drop, fear diminishes. This is as true in life as it is in surfing. The fear of what we're afraid to commit to lessens only after we've made the commitment.

Fear will never be completely gone from our lives and our work. After seven years of surfing, I still wrestle with fear. It's usually when I've been out of the water for a few too many days in a row. I hesitate on the drop, I hold back, and above all, I overthink the process—so much so that one day the guy in the water next to me said, "Need to smoke some weed . . . chill out." It made me laugh. You can easily become paralyzed by fear on the drop. Paralysis and overanalysis equal a low wave count. But without exception, when I do catch a wave, fear transforms into pure joy. You don't get to experience the thrill of riding a wave without confronting fear in the drop. They're inseparable. So just go for it, *despite* your fear.

HOW TO HAVE A MOMENT OF CREATIVE DARING

Filmmaker Brad Montague has been in the habit of making things ever since he was a child, and describes himself as an "accidental filmmaker . . . who feels like a kid who has been invited to the grown-ups' table." Brad's moment of creative daring took place when he and his wife started a weeklong camp in which to teach kids how they could change the world. He discovered kids who were building apps, starting nonprofits, and doing things he couldn't fathom doing at their age. Encouraged by all that he was seeing, he unleashed a tsunami of thoughts and ideas:

Kids should be in charge.

Kids should run this camp.

A kid should be a president. In fact, Robby, my brother-in-law, should be president.

With no exact idea in mind, Brad made a cardboard backdrop, put a record player on a desk, used a tin can for a phone, and put a presidential name tag on his brother-in-law. In an episode of the *Unmistakable Creative,* Brad recounted,

The minute he got behind the desk he started just dancing. It was perfect. It wasn't something I asked him to do. Then I began to ask him questions about how he felt about certain things. And it was such fun. We were laughing a lot. I cut together a video, and I realized I still had an hour of footage. So I cut together two more videos. I realized that there was something to the two of us playing together, the idea that I would ask him questions, and he would respond, or I would ask him to say something and he would say it in a much better way, in this honest spirited delivery.

Brad and Robby's "kidding around" was the impetus for what eventually became the viral sensation Kid President, which has reached millions of viewers around the world.

Every day we have creative impulses, moments that could make our work unmistakable. They are moments in which we feel deeply compelled to make something simply because we want to see it exist. But we're quick to write off such moments as silly. Too often, if they don't serve as a means to an end we fail to see their value. Yet it's in exactly these kinds of moments that the biggest breakthroughs occur.

When Brad started filming the Kid President videos, he couldn't have possibly known that his work would have such far-reaching impact. But that didn't stop him from picking up his camera in a moment of creative daring and hitting "record." It's a moment that has changed not only his life, but the lives of everyone his work has touched.

In a moment of creative daring we commit to the act of creating, believing the impossible is possible. Our deepest, most heartfelt work comes to fruition. It's the kind of work that invigorates and energizes us, making us want to do more and more of it. As the surfing legend Rabbit Kekai said, "Once the surfing bug bit you, you can never leave, when you feel the sand between your toes, you can never leave." The same is true when the bug of creative daring bites you.

The reality of a moment of creative daring is that the conditions will never be perfect, you'll never have all your ducks in a row. Regardless of what your current situation is, you have to have a bias toward action. I've had no business starting or managing many of the projects I've launched, like running events and complex media productions, because I didn't know anything about them. But every step forward revealed a next move that would enable me to see a project or idea to completion.

Hesitating on the Drop

Sometime in my third year of surfing, I'd gotten in the habit of hesitating on the drop. I would start to paddle, and the moment I saw the rideable section of the wave, known as the face, I would pull my board back. I couldn't get myself to go. I knew that on the other side of my fear was an epic ride. But for some reason the drop looked too big, too intimidating, and I kept envisioning a watery grave. My fear was pretty irrational, because I'd ridden thousands of waves by then. The surf wasn't particularly big either; I'd ridden far bigger waves before.

One day, after several weeks of paralysis, only one other guy was in the water. I was telling him how much I had been struggling and how I'd been letting wave after wave go by. He said, "You have to just go. And the wipeout is nowhere near as bad as you've probably made it up to be in your head." As the next set started, the voice of fear in my head was still loud and clear. I was going to lose the respect of the only other person in the lineup. My nerves were completely rattled, but if I didn't go for one of these waves, it would be another week of lots of water time with hardly any rides. I finally paddled like hell and went for wave after wave. I certainly ate shit on a few. But that day the wipeout was more important than catching waves because I finally understood it was nowhere near as bad as I thought it was going to be. I also realized that the more waves you go for, the more you'll catch. I haven't been completely paralyzed in the water since then.

Sometimes all it takes is a word of encouragement to stop hesitating on the drop, to help us understand the difference between being scared to death and scared to fail. Chances are you're scared to fail, scared to wipe out, but you're not going to die. So look for the friend in the lineup who says, "Just go."

Like the lizard brain of resistance, you'll have to face the drop when you get back in the water tomorrow. You'll have to conquer your fear, you'll have to calm your nerves, and you'll have to just go. But do it once and you'll find it in yourself to do it over and over again until not hesitating on the drop becomes a part of your identity. Surfing, or the process of becoming unmistakable, becomes an unshakable addiction and an unwavering commitment to this temperamental love affair that you have with the ocean, or creativity.

Unmistakable Creative: Robert Kurson

Robert Kurson is an American author, best known for his 2004 bestselling book Shadow Divers, *the true story of two Americans who discover a World War II German U-boat sunk sixty miles off the coast of New Jersey. Kurson began his career as an attorney, graduating from Harvard Law School and practicing real estate law. His professional writing career began at the* Chicago Sun-Times, *where he started as a sports data clerk and soon gained a full-time job writing features. He moved from the* Sun-Times *to* Chicago *magazine, then to* Esquire, *where he won a National Magazine Award and was a contributing editor for years. His stories have appeared in* Rolling Stone, *the* New York Times Magazine, *and other publications. His most recent book,* Pirate Hunters, *is about the hunt for lost gold, bitter rivalries on the high seas, a long-ago legendary pirate captain, and two adventurous American men.*

Conventional wisdom would be to stay at a high-paying job as a Harvard-educated lawyer and not start your career over from scratch as a data entry clerk at a newspaper. But conventional wisdom doesn't result in unmistakable work. Robert had never been trained as a professional writer and as a result had to learn to work without a formula or a map. His countless childhood road trips with his raconteur father gave him a unique understanding of the DNA of a compelling story, sparked his curiosity to tell his own stories, and ultimately let him find his unmistakable voice.

The earliest parts of Robert's life didn't indicate that he was destined for success of any kind. He was close to dead last in his graduating class, but the possibility of writing for the University of Wisconsin's newspaper gave him a potential inroad, so he wrote to the school: "My home life hasn't been very happy. I haven't been able to concentrate on school but if you give me probation, I'm sure I can come through."

He was admitted on probation, got straight A's, and was later accepted to Harvard Law School. Despite how far he had come since high school, he was disillusioned when he arrived at Harvard.

"Within thirty-six hours I knew I had made a horrendous mistake," he recalls. "I could tell even before classes started that this was not the place for me, that the people who would be happiest here were people who dotted every i and crossed every t and for whom order and carefulness ruled the day. But I stuck it out and became a lawyer and that's where the disaster really began."

The desire for safety and security can keep us stuck in undesirable situations. We'll frequently choose to tolerate the unfulfilling over the uncomfortable. And we do so at a very high price: the cost of our joy and self-expression. But this might also become the catalyst for a much-needed change, as it did for Robert.

Unhappiness as a Lucky Break

"Maxed out on ramen noodles and peanut butter sandwiches and dreaming of being able to afford pepperoni on my pizzas," Robert began his career as a Harvard-educated lawyer. And he found that he was instantly more miserable than he had been in law school.

"How am I going to live the next fifty years hating my job and being bad in it?" he asked himself. "I had all kinds of stuff that I had dreamed of having: a BMW, a $3,000 bicycle, a $2,000 stereo. I was never a person who used alcohol or drugs but I bought as much junk as I could to numb the pain. Nothing worked."

When we're desperately unhappy, it ironically puts us in a place of tremendous power. When we feel as if we have nothing to lose, it can become the impetus for a strong bias toward action and the beginnings of our route to unmistakable.

Flow and the DNA of Story

What never left Robert was his absolute love for telling and listening to stories. Having grown up taking long road trips with his father, who owned a motorcycle paint and lubricant company, Robert's sense of how a good story should sound was driven by the question "Is this the kind of thing that I would like to listen to on a car ride from Chicago to Milwau-

kee?" To get "through the nights, the Monday nights and the Tuesday nights and worst of all the Sunday nights," he started to write short stories about taking road trips with his dad to Northeastern Illinois University basketball games to watch a great local player, anything that reminded him of the past. And in the process of writing, he found flow.

"An incredible thing happened while I was writing those stories. Time moved very, very quickly. I would say, 'I can't believe I wrote a story in twenty-five minutes.' Then I'd look up at the clock and it'd been three hours. At the law job, time moved almost backward for me."

His lack of formal instruction in writing gave him a significant advantage in the process of developing an unmistakable voice. "It seemed to me that everyone who made their living at writing had been instructed in it. Everything depends on structure, but I wasn't able to say, 'There's going to be a beginning, a middle, and an end and a conflict at this point and then I'm going to do this later.' I quickly found that I sounded different from a lot of writers, which was an advantage. I didn't have a certain approach set in stone."

Lack of formal instruction might keep us from attempting some sort of creative pursuit or starting anything in which we don't have experience. The story of how Robert Kurson became a writer shows us that lack of experience can be turned into an advantage. When we lack experience, we also have the advantage of lacking preconceived notions of what's possible.

Defining Unmistakable

"I read an article not long ago about people who write hit songs for current pop artists. They have a formula for how they do it. I can hear this formula whenever I'm in the frozen yogurt place, the same songs playing over and over. I think that's the worst way to go about it," Kurson explained when I asked him what he thinks unmistakable means. "If you hear something from your heart, and you hear other people expressing from their heart and not from a formula, not something designed to sell a certain number of albums but because the person has to say it and they believe it, then it's unmistakable."

Kurson continued, "If people connect with who they really are inside, and transmit that, whether they are talking about themselves or talking about something as mundane as building a highway, it's unmistakable. It may not appeal to everyone, but to those to whom it also speaks, it is unmistakable."

PART FOUR:
THE RIDE

In December every year, the best surfers in the world compete at the Banzai Pipeline on the North Shore of Oahu. The waves are fast, powerful, hollow, terrifying: more people have died surfing it than anywhere else.

If you watch any surf documentary about the North Shore, you'll hear surfers say, "If you want to get noticed, this is the place." Professional surfing careers are made on the North Shore. Photographers, surf companies, magazines, and everybody else in the world of surfing gathers here to find talented surfers in the lineup. With so many great surfers chasing so many amazing waves, you'd better be able to rip (surfer lingo for performing at a high level).

Creators, entrepreneurs, and artists who want to master their craft are attempting to surf a version of the Banzai Pipeline. We want to get to our own North Shore and ride the biggest wave of our lives. With so many people starting projects, we'd better be able to rip.

Our tolerance for mediocrity today is virtually zero. People want art by masters of their craft, employers want only to hire experts, and other masters want to work with those who have the potential for mastery. If we're mediocre, even if we manage to catch a wave, we'll struggle to stay on our boards, lose our balance, and what might have been a perfect ride will end in a wipeout.

In an interview on the *Off Camera* podcast, host Sam Jones asked actor Ed Helms (the nerdy guy with glasses in the *Hangover* movies who became well known in *The Office*) about his thoughts on success after becoming so famous that he's recognized on the streets. He said that "life is a series of false horizons," which stuck with me. On the path to mastery, nearly every external marker of success is a false horizon. Those who have yet to master a craft assume there will be some moment of arrival, an "I've made it" moment. Because it's easier than ever to start something, mastery of your craft is more critical than ever. Masters of a craft are lifelong learners. They never settle. Every single ride takes a surfer one step closer to mastery. Each evolution, each progression is a false horizon because the challenges that the ocean presents to a surfer are infinite.

Putting on a wetsuit, renting a surfboard, and jumping in the water is the easy part. But learning to ride and developing your style takes effort and time. At the place I surf in San Clemente, California, I run into guys who have surfed for more than forty years—longer than most people have careers—who tell great stories of the days when the water wasn't crowded and when they didn't surf with leashes. These guys can rip. They raise the bar in the lineup. But what I love most about talking to them is that they're still learning to surf. The power and temperament of the ocean breeds humility and respect. They're committed to the ride.

You never stop learning how to surf, and masters never stop learning their craft. For surfers, our love affair with the ocean goes from our first wave to the grave, and for masters of their craft it's a commitment from their first piece of work to the end of their lives. Only through this kind of dedication do we have any chance at mastery. In order to achieve mastery of the ride, we have to understand the actions, habits, and characteristics of the masters who have come before us.

According to author Robert Greene, who has written best-selling books like *Mastery* and *The 48 Laws of Power,* mastery is a combination of the rational and the intuitive. Many of us can take a rational approach, develop our skills, and perform with proficiency. We can study those who have gone before us. We can put in the necessary practice time. But this alone won't make us unmistakable. For example, hundreds of YouTube videos reveal violinists playing difficult violin concertos. Through a significant amount of practice, they can master the mechanics. But what distinguishes those who are deemed unmistakable masters is the ability to perform at the highest level while *also* bringing their own absolutely individual interpretation to a piece of music. The *intuitive* is our style, our fingerprint, the little but important difference that makes us unmistakable.

Unmistakable mastery doesn't lie in our ability to replicate or imitate a performance. It lies in our ability to adapt what we've learned and make it our own. The kid who can play the *Guitar Hero* video game impeccably is not unmistakable. The one who can perform his own songs with the same skill is unmistakable.

Mastery occurs at the fusion of performance at the highest level, the rational, with style, the intuitive.

When our motivation is purely extrinsic, we have no shot at

mastery. If we don't experience the external rewards, we fail to see the value in the activity. But when our motivation is also intrinsic, the activity itself provides a tremendous sense of value and personal fulfillment. Because of that we can commit the time, energy, and effort required for mastery. We see our work not as a chore, but as an opportunity to play. As Steven Kotler wrote in his book *The Rise of Superman,* "No one has to drag a surfer out of bed for overhead tubes [big waves that make a surfer feel as if he's inside a tunnel made of water]. No one has to motivate a snowboarder on a powder day. These activities are intrinsically motivating, autotelic experiences done for their own sake. The high to end all highs."

An added benefit to intrinsic motivation is that it causes all aspects of performance to go through the roof, paving the way for us to become unmistakable masters of our craft.

- *Writers shape words into poetic sentences that we can't help but be moved by.*

- *Musicians push the limits of technical proficiency with their instruments.*

- *Athletes go from average to extraordinary. Basketball players don't miss shots, baseball players hit home runs, and surfers ride the biggest waves imaginable.*

The quality of work and the caliber of our skill are drastically enhanced by intrinsic motivation.

But this dramatic increase in the quality of our work is

never the by-product of one moment, one decision to create, one decision to act, one decision to go for a wave. Each creation to an artist is a fraction of a larger body of work. One blog post, one piece of music, or one book does not define an entrepreneur, musician, or author; rather, it's the cumulative output and experience that ultimately determine both your level of mastery and how unmistakable you will become.

DELIBERATE PRACTICE

In the summer of 2009, after finishing my MBA, I was unemployed and became completely obsessed with surfing. As a result, I logged an unusually high amount of water time for someone who had never surfed. From July until December I was in the water for nearly six hours a day. Because it's free and takes up so much time, I say that surfing is the perfect hobby for an unemployed person.

I didn't realize it while it was happening, but the insane amount of time I was spending in the water was an incredibly deep voyage of self-discovery, forcing me to examine my life and do everything in my power to ensure that I never again worked at an unfulfilling job.

One pivotal moment during those six months made the difference between continuing my crisis of mediocrity and pursuing the unmistakable. In late October 2009, I actually found a job. One week into the job, I had an eerily familiar feeling. I dreaded the days, my stomach was hurting, my lunch breaks and my six-hour surf sessions had been reduced to one hour. Even during the initial interview, one of the staff warned, "Your surfing days will be over soon."

The Thursday of the second week at that job, at two p.m., I shut down my laptop and walked out the door, without looking back. And the next morning I was at the beach.

Even after I found another job in January 2010, I made it a point to surf from six a.m. to eight a.m. every morning and I would spend from eight a.m. to two p.m. in the water on the weekends. As a result, I progressed faster than I had at almost anything else I'd done in my life. When I was let go from my last day job in 2011, I temporarily moved to Costa Rica because of its reputation for warm water and perfect waves, and I surfed three hours every morning and three hours every evening for six months.

I didn't realize it, but I was learning to surf through deliberate practice. Deliberate practice is addictive. It causes the kind of exhaustion that makes you smile because you know you've done some of the most unmistakable work of your life.

In the 2005 film *Coach Carter,* Samuel L. Jackson plays Ken Carter, based on a real-life high school basketball coach at Richmond High School in California. In the movie, when Carter first arrives at the school, he says, "I cannot teach you the game of basketball until your conditioning is at a level that allows me to do so." The rigorous and brutal workouts he designs for his team are a great example of deliberate practice. A significant amount of the players' training doesn't involve actually playing basketball but rather conditioning through a series of strenuous exercises.

In the first practice Carter had the team run "suicides" for one hour and seven minutes. According to Betterbasketball coaching.com, a suicide is "a conditioning drill that simulates the start-stop action of a real basketball game, and is a great way to build up anaerobic power for the sprinting that happens in the game." Each sprint is longer than the previous one. Carter pushed his players beyond what they thought was physically possible. He required every member of the team to do hundreds of pushups at every practice. When the team's free throw rate was only 56 percent, he made every player stay at practice until they made fifty free throws.

The result of this torturous routine? The team went from a losing record to being undefeated within one year. With deliberate practice, drastic improvements start to occur over an incredibly short time line. That's the power of deliberate practice.

Deliberate practice, habit, and ritual help German visual artist Mars Dorian master his craft. Dorian looks at images and artworks on social media networks like Pinterest, which are full of illustrations, animations, and creative photographs from artists around the world. "This helps me to get inspired and opens my mind for my own work," Mars explains. "I then plug in my Wacom tablet Intuos4, a drawing pad that allows me to paint digitally. I start the actual drawing/design work only when it's dark outside. My studio is noisy during the daytime. Also, at night, my brain isn't so active anymore, which means the unconscious takes over and allows for more unrestricted, creative flow. After the warmup sketching, I do the actual design work while listening to electronic music without lyrics. I need music to perform, it puts me into a trance that helps with the work. I then work till I'm too tired to lift my pen or the sun knocks on my window. Rinse and repeat."

Like Carter's basketball team, Mars's practice consists of more than just drawing. He looks at the work of other artists, warms up, listens to music, and starts the actual drawing and designing. When I asked him how long he had been drawing for upward of three hours a day, he said it was more than twenty years. If you look closely at the story of Mars Dorian, you'll notice a pattern that emerges in nearly all masters of their craft. His work is dictated entirely by ritual, of which deliberate practice forms a daily part, and that ritual continues over the time that Mars has committed to mastering his craft.

A master such as Mars doesn't question the value of working at his art.

In his now iconic 2011 documentary *Jiro Dreams of Sushi*, filmmaker David Gelb profiled the Japanese chef Jiro Ono. As the movie opens Jiro says, "You must dedicate your life to mastering your skill." His commitment to his craft is so serious that he has no plans to retire until he's physically or mentally incapable of working. He commits to being exceptional at one thing. When patrons come into the restaurant to ask if they serve appetizers or sake, they're informed that the restaurant serves only sushi.

Effort and repetition play an instrumental role in how Jiro prepares sushi. He repeats the same exact routine and ritual every day. He boards the subway from the same exact position. With every single piece of sushi he serves, he aims to improve on the one before. A food writer named Masuhiro Yamamoto describes the characteristics that make Jiro a great chef:

- *Takes the work seriously*
- *Aspires to improve*
- *Cleanliness*
- *Impatience*
- *Passion*

Multiple decades of practice have gone into Jiro's work as a chef. His love for sushi borders on obsessive (he's literally having dreams about preparing it). Every piece of fish is like a wave, and every moment in the kitchen, time in the water.

The standards to which Jiro commits have caused many of his apprentices to last no more than a day. Like Carter and Mars, Jiro goes beyond the preparation and serving of the sushi. His meticulousness and commitment bleed into every aspect of his life and his work. While your obsession doesn't have to be as extreme as Jiro's, you can and should hold yourself to an incredibly high standard in your work.

When we commit to the pursuit of mastery and engage in deliberate practice, according to author Geoff Colvin, we are engaging in an activity just beyond our current ability. If the activity is within our comfort zone, we don't experience any growth and we can even become bored. Often this happens to people in jobs that are repetitive, mundane, and don't challenge them in any way. You may have had this experience. If the activity is too difficult, we get frustrated. In between the two is a sweet spot, our unmistakable zone, or flow.

In this sweet spot of flow, we bring a heightened sense of awareness and interest to our work. We welcome challenges. We see them as opportunities for growth rather than obstacles. As our skill increases, the boundaries of our ability continually expand. Our deliberate practice, therefore, must also be constantly retooled and updated. It's difficult, if not impossible, to figure out each day exactly what practice will challenge but not frustrate us.

Dr. Jeff Spencer has worked with Olympic gold medalists, champion athletes, and world-class achievers in nearly every field. Jeff uses the term "evolutionary pacing" to describe practice at a level just beyond our current level of ability. We must pace ourselves based on where we are at and incrementally expose ourselves to readiness for the next level of our performance. If we try to outrun our pacing, we'll fail to reach technical proficiency. If somewhere in the process of developing technical proficiency we cultivate bad habits, our foundation will become faulty and our potential will be limited later in our development. When I asked him about the deliberate practice of gold medal winners, he listed the following critical factors:

- *Sport-specific conditioning*
- *Agility*
- *Recovery*
- *Good nutrition*
- *Good sleep*

- *Recreation and great fellowship*
- *Time away from the activity itself*

Notice that the sport-specific conditioning is only one element of the practice. Preparation for the activity is as critical as the activity itself. In other words, deliberate practice involves much more than working on whatever craft we're trying to master. While the routine above is specific to sports, it's a framework that you could apply to mastering any endeavor, whatever your craft might be.

You probably are a long way from achieving mastery. But in this moment you have two choices: decide that you're simply not destined to become masterful at anything, *or* commit to mastering your craft. So how do we keep moving in the direction of mastery? With a little help from our friends.

MENTORS, COACHES, AND FEEDBACK

I was in a yoga class when I realized that nonpretzel humans can't do all the poses. Apparently, if you can't do the poses, the instructor will come over and hand you a block. Sometimes you just have to ask for a block. You need to realize that you might need help. This was such a profound insight for me in that moment in yoga class.

Anything of great significance is accomplished with the help of other people. A coach, mentor, or collaborator plays an integral role in the path to mastery. In some cases this role is informal: a teacher or boss takes an interest in us. In other cases, we purposely seek out someone. As founder of the Ultimate Game of Life, Jim Bunch said in an episode of the *Unmistakable Creative* podcast, "Coaches have an amazing way of taking interest in people, seeing those people for better than what they are and moving them in a new direction." Because we are so close to our work, it can be hard to see ourselves for "better than what we are" and accurately assess our development. The right coach or mentor can teach us how to build an effective foundation, create daily habits, and shift our thinking a little bit at a time. As a result, a coach or mentor can drastically accelerate our progress toward becoming unmistakable.

Think about these three main questions when considering a mentor:

- *Has this person gotten the result that you're seeking?*
- *Has this person helped someone else achieve the result you're seeking?*
- *Is this the right coach for you based on where you're at in your evolution?*

For a long time I resisted asking for help on how to grow my podcast's audience and revenue. After all, I had access to the brightest minds of our time and could ask them anything I wanted in an interview. But at a certain point I realized that while they provided insights and motivation, I wanted to sit down with someone, go over specific questions I had, and get some very personalized advice. That was when I turned to a former podcast guest. I met Greg Hartle in 2010 when he started a project called Ten Dollars and a Laptop. The premise was simple: visit all fifty states, work one-on-one with five hundred people, and start a business. The caveat was that the only two resources he could use were his laptop and ten dollars, nothing else. I was one of those fortunate five hundred people.

Greg had asked me to become director of marketing for a company he co-owned. Given my track record of being fired from every job I'd had, I resisted. On the other hand, I figured anybody who could visit all fifty states with nothing but ten dollars and a laptop had to be the most resourceful human being I could know. I jokingly refer to him as the "Jack Bauer of the Internet." So I told him I'd agree on the condition that he would mentor me in the growth of my business. With Greg's coaching, I made more progress in six months than I had in two years.

- *He taught me how to run my podcast as a real business (including using a corporate bank account and profit-and-loss statements).*

- *He taught me about the importance of reviewing metrics, goals, and progress toward those goals on a weekly basis.*

- *He had the foresight to see we needed to develop a brand identity. He was the one who came up with the name Unmistakable Creative.*

- *Under his guidance, we planned and executed the sold-out Instigator Experience conference.*

Some people have such a profound impact on our lives that they completely alter the course of them. Sometimes we recognize them only in retrospect. By knowing that these kinds of people play a role in the path to mastery, we can be on the lookout for them and recognize them when they show up.

As a young aspiring author, Dani Shapiro attended Sarah Lawrence College, where she met the American short story writer Grace Paley. On her blog, Shapiro writes:

> I remember, as a freshman at Sarah Lawrence, the first time I wound up on the floor of Grace's office. You didn't sit in chairs around Grace. Everything somehow ended up grounded and earthy—she was a powerful maternal presence. We students curled up in her lap—sometimes literally—or lounged on pillows on her office floor, safe in her capacious embrace. To be with her was to learn. I remember things she told me. She told me I was a writer. She told me I should stay at Sarah Lawrence and go to graduate school. She helped to make that happen.

Dani Shapiro has made her living as a writer for more than twenty years. She's the author of three memoirs and five novels. Her work has appeared in *The New Yorker,* and she's been on Oprah's *SuperSoul Sunday.* It's possible she would have been successful without her mentor, but it's clear Grace Paley was an influential figure in her life. The dedication of her most recent book *Still Writing* reads, "In Memory of Grace Paley."

A Bank Robber Who Mentored a Bestselling Author

Sometimes we find mentors in the most unexpected ways. Piper Kerman, author of the book *Orange Is the New Black,* which was turned into an Emmy Award–winning Netflix series, hardly fits the profile of someone you'd expect to find in prison. She was a college graduate with a career, boyfriend, and loving family. But ten years after delivering a suitcase full of drug money, her past caught up with her and she ended up serving fifteen months in a federal prison.

While she was incarcerated, she found a mentor in *Unmistakable Creative* guest Joe Loya, who had robbed thirty banks. Loya sent his book *The Man Who Outgrew His Prison Cell: Confessions of a Bank Robber* to her and they began a correspondence. Given his own experience with serving time, he had a profound understanding of what she was dealing with. In a conversation on our podcast he said: "I told Piper, 'Listen, all your friends love you and all of them know you better than I do, but none of them know what I know you've been going through right now.' She would ask me things, she would tell me things, and I would encourage her. You can talk to strangers different and that's how our friendship grew. I told her, 'Write a book. You need to write the stuff down every night. Write something funny that happened to you that you heard and write something sad or dark that you heard.'"

Our mentors don't always come dressed in suits and working in corner offices.

STYLE: THE NO-BULLSHIT YOU

Beginning surfers are often taught on a large, foam, soft-top board, used to prevent injuries. The design of the board is inherently limited. It provides stability, buoyancy, and the ability to easily stand up and ride a wave. But it lacks flexibility and maneuverability. So a surfer "graduates" from the soft-top to a real board. The real board allows for the ability to do tricks, turns, and the subtle variations that bring style to the ride. When we graduate to a real board, surfing becomes our art, the wave becomes our canvas, and the ride becomes our unmistakable signature.

The process of selecting a wave, making the drop, and standing up on the board becomes unconscious to a surfer. He doesn't have to think about it because he's put in so much water time and ridden so many waves. Because of the body of knowledge he's accumulated, he's able to rely on and tap into his intuition to bring style to the way he rides a wave. Same goes with your unmistakable art when you've committed to the ride.

At some point, a surfer's style becomes so distinctive that we can spot him from the shore by the way he rides. I've even noticed a few of my friends who surf develop their own distinctive styles. In a sea of wetsuits I can easily pick them out of the lineup by watching them ride one wave. The style, the flair, the thing that they bring to a wave, makes them unmistakable.

As creators, we graduate to a "real board" when we move

beyond the rational and start to depend on intuition. We have a large body of research and know-how to rely on, but we don't rely on it solely. We move from mechanics, capable of repeating a process over and over, graduating to artists capable of infusing what we feel deeply compelled to be, do, or say into our work. Style in any art form emerges when we let go of what we perceive as universal truth and start to embrace what is true for us. Our art must answer deeper questions of what makes us feel completely alive, what we want to be known for, and how we want to be remembered. Our foundational habits and our mentors and coaches have served as training wheels. Now it's time for us to make the ride our own.

Even though we are at an advanced stage in our practice, discovering our style paradoxically requires us to be in a much more childlike, primitive, and inquisitive state. As author Erik Wahl says, we must return to a place "when curiosity ruled our senses" and "enthusiasm ignited our actions." We must make a shift from "I know what will happen" to "What would happen if . . . ?" We have to embrace mystery. This requires us to trust our intuition more than rational thought. But trusting our intuition can't be reduced to a five-step formula that leads to an unmistakable style. It's different for each of us.

When developing our style, we must learn to experiment. Like a master chef who throws an ingredient into a recipe to change the flavor of a dish after refining his palate through years of practice, we must keep trying new ingredients in our work. Using Korean barbecue in a taco was unheard of, but it's exactly what the founders of the Kogi BBQ taco truck in Los

Angeles did. When they tweeted their location, the lines were upward of an hour long. The only reason I was ever able to try one of their tacos is because we hired them to cater an event.

When I wanted to mix two different artistic styles on the *Unmistakable Creative* Web site, my mentor questioned my judgment. Greg wasn't sure that combining such different artists would be effective. This approach would never have occurred to me without the sheer variety of creators and artists I'd been exposed to throughout the years that I'd been working: the combination of the intuitive and the rational. I felt they would make the site unmistakable.

Big breakthroughs occur when we are willing to challenge conventional wisdom. How could you change one small ingredient of your work that might make a difference in your style? For example:

If you're a photographer, use light in a creative way.

If you're a blogger, explore the vulnerable edges of your work and say what you've been afraid to say. Let your prose turn into poetry.

If you're an artist, try a color or a medium you've never used before.

If you're a filmmaker, add a scene that's not in the script.

As we continually make small changes, our intuition becomes more refined, until we trust it completely. As a result, our art becomes unmistakable, requiring no signature.

The interviews I conduct on the *Unmistakable Creative* podcast are largely unscripted, with the exception of a few questions that I feel compelled to ask in every interview. Like the surfer who doesn't have to think about the process of choosing a wave and standing up on it, I don't have to consciously think about how to conduct an interview. I take the conversation in the direction in which I feel it will have the greatest impact on someone listening. My ability to navigate a conversation with somebody I barely know is based on intuition that is the product of the hundreds of conversations I've had before.

Review Your Work and Ask for Feedback

While repetition will certainly hone your intuition, you must also consume and review your own work. Because of our small staff, and the fact that I get to review my work, I still edit every interview myself, so I end up listening to each interview three times: once when I'm actually conducting the interview, a second time when I'm editing it, and a third time after it's been published. I make notes of questions I wish I had asked, threads that I would have dug deeper into, and more. I also take feedback from our listeners into consideration.

While I was writing this book, a listener sent in an e-mail saying that he loved the show but found the use of some filler language like "let me ask you . . ." really annoying. Initially I rolled my eyes, but when I went back and listened to an episode I heard how right he was. Every time I heard the phrase I cringed. I said it so many times in one interview that I e-mailed him back to say thank you and that I would work on it. Now I'm hyperaware of any moment when I'm tempted to say that.

- *If you're a writer, go back and read the things you've written. You might consider even rewriting them entirely.*
- *If you're a singer, record your sessions and listen to them.*
- *If you own a company, look back at previous versions of your product (an app, a piece of clothing, etc.) and make notes of how you could improve it.*

One of the fringe benefits to reviewing what you've already created is that you will improve in the future while also getting ideas for new things to create, enabling you to leverage repetition.

Style in Practice

Developing style means your work will not be liked by everybody. But people naturally want to be liked. So we avoid polarizing points of view. We hide a lot of things from the world out of fear—fear of being judged, fear of being criticized, fear of being ridiculed. We must be willing to be wrong. We must come to terms with the idea that we are not who we thought we were. When we're honest, raw, and open, we connect, we touch people, we put out a signal into the world to the right people.

When Howard Stern began his career in radio, he pushed a lot of buttons. In a telling scene in the documentary *Private Parts,* the program director is discussing Stern's ratings with somebody on the research staff. The average person who loved Stern listened for an hour. Those who hated him? Two hours. Both groups said they wanted to hear what he would say next. In 2014, music critic Bob Lefsetz wrote about Stern's success:

> *Everybody rubs off the rough edges, they believe if they don't appeal to everybody, they're not going to appeal to anybody. But the truth is long-term careers are based on being unique, trailblazing in your own world. . . . Becky G worked with Dr. Luke and ended up sounding just like everybody else, how she lost her edge, and that's what we've got in music, everybody sounds the same, except for those without enough talent. They're afraid to go their own way, afraid radio won't play them and the media won't feature them. But unless you have the confidence to woodshed in the wilderness until you're appealing to the masses you'll never become a legend.*

While sanding off the rough edges of your work might make you agreeable, and even somewhat likable, it's not a recipe for unmistakable. In fact, the rough edges are where your most unmistakable elements lie.

Myth: if you don't appeal to everybody, you won't appeal to anybody.

Truth: if you try to appeal to everybody, you'll appeal to nobody.

In the early part of his career, Stern played it safe and did what was expected. He avoided anything too edgy. Not until he embraced his rough edges did he start to connect with his audience.

Ashley Ambirge embodies what it means to have style. In a sea of copywriters who promise outcomes like conversions, clear mission statements, and other monotonous corporate drivel, her company, House of Moxie, and her blog, *The Middle Finger Project,* is filled with "irreverent thoughts, bold advice and new ideas for entrepreneurs." When I asked her about voice, she said something that has always stayed with me: You want to "hit people in the face with a crowbar." Heard out of context it sounds like something out of a prison yard. But for Ashley Ambirge, using every word to hit people in the face with a crowbar is what sets her work apart. In a post she writes:

> *If you want to stand out, feel fresh, appear interesting and get noticed . . . then you've got to use language that stands out, feels fresh, is interesting and gets noticed.*
>
> *This is common sense, but of course, it's easier said than done. It's tempting to use the first words that come to your mind, but usually? Those are the last words that'll make you stand out from anyone else's. This is why good copywriting is so important. The cutesy, overused, cliché phrases have gotta go. Ditto this shitty coffee. WHY AM I STILL DRINKING SHITTY COFFEE?*

1. Guru
2. Manifesto

3. Solutions

4. Empowerment

5. Juicy

6. Rock (out) (on) (your world) (etc.)

7. Fempreneur (This one's for you, J.)

8. Thrive

9. Alchemist

10. Luminary (seriously?)

11. Epic

12. Shiny

13. Sexy

14. e-Book

15. Kick ass

16. Domination

17. Insanely _____.

18. Ridiculously _____.

19. Killer

20. Rocket science

21. Laser-focused

22. Freakin'

23. Bucket list

24. Remarkable

25. Newsletter

Please. If nothing else, ditch newsletter. *This is a plea. A petition. And maybe even a* prayer. *Nobody is chomping at the bit to sign up for anybody's "newsletter." I'm not saying not to send (an incredibly well-thought out + useful one)—I'm saying that* this is not the language that gets results. *And language is* everything.

Vulnerability, great writing, grace—and profanity—give Ashley a provocative, absolutely unmistakable style and voice. Your temptation after reading that might be to create a cocktail of vulnerability and f-bombs in the hopes of cutting through the noise the way Ashley does. But the lesson to take away from the work of someone like Ashley is to be unapologetically yourself.

Provocativeness for no good reason (e.g., posting nude pictures, making sex tapes, or using gratuitous profanity) doesn't make our style unmistakable. We must learn to be provocative with a purpose. On the flip side, being agreeable all the time will ensure that we'll never be unmistakable. In the years I've been a podcaster, blogger, entrepreneur, and multimedia producer I've been called both a disservice to humanity and a gift to the world. I've had to be willing to live with both in order to be unmistakable.

A BOX OF CRAYONS AND CREATIVE DARING

If you give a piece of paper to adults and say to draw anything, or even "draw a pair of scissors," they will take an hour, trying to capture every detail, while getting frustrated and complaining that they can't draw scissors. If you give children a blank page and a pen, tell them to draw anything, and leave the room for an hour, they will run out of paper, draw more than you asked for, and tell you a story to go along with it. Children in action overflow with creativity. Every moment, they're putting on a show. They're delighted by having the opportunity to play and create, and by their own work. That kind of enthusiasm is essential to doing work that's unmistakable.

As we grow older, I think something starts to zap these moments of creative daring out of us. We become hyper-self-aware. We start to ask the question "Does this suck?" We start to categorize ourselves into creative or not, smart or not. A big part of the spiritual journey of adulthood is unraveling all the layers that take us back to who we were in our childhood.

When you have moments of creative daring, you might be tempted to write off the result as a batshit-crazy idea with no hope for how it might become reality. But if you're willing to trust in something beyond yourself—what author Steven Pressfield calls the "quantum soup," what spiritual people refer to as the "universe"—somehow the world starts to conspire in your favor to make your idea happen. Some of the greatest art ever created, companies we can't imagine our lives without, and the most unmistakable acts, happened in moments of creative daring.

Pushing the edge, crossing your own boundaries, is exhilarating. You've managed to get out of your own way to do something unmistakable.

But it's also terrifying because . . .

- *What if everybody laughs?*
- *What if nobody cares?*

- *What if it gets ignored?*
- *What if you fail and lose money, time, and dignity?*

I've asked myself every one of those questions in my own moments of creative daring. People did laugh, people did ignore me, and I did lose time, money, and dignity.

The flip side of the moment of creative daring is:

- *What if it works?*
- *What if you exceed your own expectations?*
- *What if you stretch and grow in ways you couldn't imagine?*

For Erika Lyremark, that's exactly what happened. Erika had spent nine years working as a stripper. In 2001 she left the industry and a year later had already created a successful commercial real estate company with her father. When she left that company to start her new career as a business mentor, she wanted to shed the identity of her past as a stripper because she was afraid she wouldn't be taken seriously. Only her husband and a handful of close friends knew about her past. But she knew that she'd eventually have to tell her story or somebody else would.

After six months of working with a skilled branding consultancy, Erika finally confessed her past to her new company. According to her branding mentor, Erika's stripping experience was branding gold, a moment of creative daring. She was incredibly business savvy, intellectual, and highly creative.

So Erika started to tell some of her newer friends about her past. To her surprise, most people's reaction was overwhelmingly positive. One of those friends ran a networking group for young professionals and asked Erika to come and speak about building a personal brand. She let him know that she planned to come out about her past working as a stripper. Initially, the presentation seemed like any other, but as soon as she got to the part about working as a stripper, she grabbed the audience's attention. She recalls:

> I was really nervous that people would say really mean things to me afterward. On the flip side I knew that [my story] would really inspire some people. My whole life when I see people make bold moves I get super stoked. So after the presentation, nobody threw rotten tomatoes at me, nobody booed me, nobody tied me to a stake and lit me on fire. A lot of people came up to me afterward and congratulated me on sharing my story and told me how inspiring it was.

From that point forward Erika infused her stripping experience into her entire brand. She started pushing personal boundaries in ways that were uncomfortable. She talked about her story in presentations, on social media, and in her blog posts. Instead of hiding the story, she used it front and center in all of her work. She developed a coaching program called the Daily Whip, has mentored thousands of women around the world, and wrote a book called *Think Like a Stripper.*

We're tempted to leave out so many parts of our stories because we fear how we'll be seen or judged. I thought talking about how I had been fired from just about every job I've ever had would be career suicide. But it wasn't until I started talking about the things that scared me that my work truly started to resonate with people. Who would have thought that the stories of getting fired would be the catalyst for reaching the next level in my career? These parts of ourselves expose our humanity, showing the world that we're flawed, which paradoxically connects with people. A moment of creative daring is a no-bullshit expression of who you are.

A few years ago, I went for a walk on a Sunday morning in Riverside, California. My mind was brewing ideas like a coffee barista. The ideas were no longer blog posts or books or information products. In my head I was hatching an event unlike anything else. The idea started out as the "Unusual Suspects," a conference without the standard speaker lineup. But I later found out that the domain name for "Unusual Suspects" would cost $1,000.

I started to think back to all the conversations I'd had over several hundred interviews, and one in particular resurfaced that morning. Lisa Gansky, cofounder of the photo sharing site Ofoto and author of *The Mesh,* had told me that the world we live in was breeding two kinds of creators: entrepreneurs and instigators. Then she said, "You're an instigator." By some definitions "instigator" is a bad thing. A class clown can be an instigator. A person who prevents a group of people from reaching a successful outcome can be an instigator.

But it can also mean someone who initiates a project. The Unusual Suspects didn't have quite the same ring to it as the Instigator Experience. So I did a search for the domain name and theinstigatorexperience.com was available at the standard price of $9.99. Coming up with that name and acting on my intuition was a moment of creative daring that would ultimately lead to the event that I'm most proud of. In a moment of creative daring we have to be open to all the possibilities that might arise. I could have scrapped my idea when the domain I wanted wasn't available. If we're flexible, creative, and resourceful, a moment of creative daring can ultimately lead to what we want. I wanted an event that had none of the usual suspects (i.e., household names and people who seem to be on the roster of every conference) as speakers and still be a big success, and that's exactly what I ended up with.

Meanwhile, in the summer of 2013, one of my team members had mastered the art of creating beautiful presentations that went viral on the social media site SlideShare. From watching him, I developed an eye for typography and layout. I also started to notice the work that many cartoonists were sharing on Facebook every day. From them, I saw how visuals could be combined with words to create something beautiful and powerful.

When I saw the effects of how visual art infused their work, I knew I wanted the visual to be part of my work too. I started a thirty-day project to teach myself how to draw. I purchased a book called *You Can Draw in 30 Days*. Every day I would spend several hours trying to sketch bottles, bananas, apples, and various household items. At the beginning of the project I would get frustrated because what I was drawing looked nothing like it did in the book. But as the project continued, I'd get lost in the process for hours and draw far more than I had planned to, finding the perfect escape. I'd get ideas for images I wanted to draw on the Internet. I'd search for YouTube videos on subjects like "how to draw an airplane." Any time I was tempted to mindlessly browse the Internet or waste time on social media, instead I would sit down and draw something.

At the start of the project I drew like a kindergartner. At the end of it I could draw like a first grader. You can see the entire project on Instagram, @unmistakableCEO. Even though I could only draw like a first grader, I was quite pleased with my progress and how I had embraced childlike curiosity. I started by drawing an apple, and finished it by attempting to draw a portrait of Steve Jobs (just a coincidence). At the moment, I'm considering starting another thirty-day drawing project with a Wacom tablet and even taking a stab at animating something.

While I never committed to the craft, I used drawing to learn to see the world in a different way. A blank page was no longer a place that could be filled with just words. It was a canvas upon which to paint the reflections of my inner self. I started to lose my inhibition throughout my creative processes as a writer and an interviewer. I asked more daring questions about people's rock bottom moments, their flaws and insecurities. I wrote like there would be no consequences to anything I expressed and stopped worrying what other people would think.

I could see the potential for art in new places. When our developer Bradley Gauthier started designing our Web site, he asked me to collect stock photography for it. The first version of UnmistakableCreative.com lacked any style or flair. I told Brad, "I don't feel anything when I see it. If I don't feel it, nobody else will." After looking at it closely, I realized that the *Unmistakable Creative* site wasn't actually unmistakable or creative. I decided that we should custom illustrate all the icons, including custom graphics by Mars Dorian. In that moment we went from launching a Web site to launching a brand. I attribute that spark of creativity and that different way of thinking to the thirty days in which I started to learn how to draw.

Today, an artistic signature that combines design, typography, and visual art permeates everything we do. In fact, we don't let anything out the door without our artistic signature.

I recommend trying a thirty-day project that has nothing to do with your work. Your only goal is progress: you should be slightly better than you were when you started. A few sample thirty-day projects that may change the way you see the world include writing something every day: a series of letters to friends, to your older self, and to your younger self. At the end of thirty days, mail them. Or write a first chapter of a novel that you've been dying to write; maybe a page a day for thirty days. Write a poem in a specific form such as a haiku, villanelle, or sestina every day.

My friend and prolific photographer Matthew Monroe suggested doing thirty days of street photography in whatever city you're living in. Photograph anything that catches your eye. Often we're so familiar with the environment we're in that we stop noticing the things around us.

Pick up a ukulele, recorder, or even guitar and take one You-Tube video lesson each day. Use your computer and record yourself playing each day. At the end of thirty days, compare day one to day thirty.

You'll be amazed at what happens. Something as simple as thirty days of drawing can turn your life inside out in an unexpected, unmistakable way.

Unmistakable Creative: Mars Dorian

Mars Dorian was the person who planted the whole idea of being unmistakable in my head. What has always blown my mind about his work is that anytime we share it, anytime I see it on the Internet, anytime I see anything he's done for another client, I have no question as to who did it. He doesn't have to put his signature on it. I think that is one of the most significant achievements any creative professional could have. That's unmistakable.

Based out of Berlin, Mars is a digital illustrator, consultant, storyteller, and author whose motto is "When you're not trying to fit in, you're free to stand out." He's designed book covers, movie posters, logos, and more for the Unmistakable Creative *and is an integral part of our brand.*

Ice Cream and Karma

Mars Dorian's calling was revealed in the strangest of ways: a childhood obsession with ice cream. He recalls the pivotal moment:

> When I was seven years old, I went to the North Sea with my parents. In a supermarket there I saw a huge box of ice cream and I was just waddling toward the box like a zombie. I was so addicted to ice cream, I was

> like an ice cream junkie. But then next to the ice cream I
> saw a stand full of magazines and comics. I had no idea
> what a comic book was but it was so colorful. I saw a
> cover that showed four guys with some kind of weapon,
> and I picked up that strange little thing, flipped the
> pages, and I was in love. It turned out to be the first comic
> book of Ghostbusters. My mother said, "So, have you
> picked your ice cream?" and I said, "Mom, I don't want ice
> cream, I want this comic." She thought I was joking.

That was the start of a new obsession, a new love affair, a new calling. He went home and started drawing and has been doing it ever since. Sometimes we have to see the comic books next to the ice cream in order to discover what we're destined to do.

Creativity as a Way Out of Darkness

After traveling the world, Mars returned to Germany with no college education. He was twenty-five. It was one of the darkest periods of his life.

> I moved back to my mother's place because I had no
> money, and that was the hardest time of my life. I was
> lying in bed until four in the afternoon. I was suicidal.
> I went to an emergency room because my outlook was
> just dark and I was not getting any better. Then a

friend said, "Why don't you start drawing again? You were so creative back in high school. Why did you give up on that? Have a Web site, do it all in English, show your stuff and blog."

That was the beginning of his return to drawing and his Web site, MarsDorian.com.

The "dark night of the soul," while painful, is also frequently the source of some of the most unmistakable art that's ever been made. Throughout history people have turned to creativity as a way of navigating difficult times in their lives. If you're in a particularly difficult chapter of your life, like Mars, some sort of creative pursuit might just be your way back into the light.

Getting Started

Because he hated the analog process of drawing and the feel of a pencil on his skin, Mars bought a graphic tablet that enabled him to draw directly on his screen. When he drew, he found himself in a state of flow: "When I got the tablet, I drew for two days straight. It changed my life. I started drawing pictures that I showed on my blog, on Twitter, Tumblr. I created a little network of like-minded bloggers and creative entrepreneurs."

Eventually his work paid off, and someone in Texas asked him to draw a mascot. Mars couldn't believe someone on the other side *of the planet was giving him money for a digital drawing. This first assignment was when his online illustration career took off.*

If you get into the continual habit of creating and sharing your unmistakable work with the world, whether that is on your own Web site, Twitter, or Tumblr, it simply can't be ignored.

The Evolution of an Unmistakable Style

To continually evolve and develop his artistic style, Mars has made the conscious effort to seek inspiration outside his comfort zone, read books that he normally would not read, and look at art styles that he normally wouldn't have any interest in, in order to expand his horizons.

> *You have to make a conscious effort to absorb inspiration from different and opposing sources. Let that sink into your subconscious so that you have a huge passive database of ideas and then when you want to create, you can indirectly leverage from the sources that you have accumulated over the years.*

By drawing from video games, various comic styles, American and Japanese pop culture, and a wide variety of art forms, he's combined influences to create work that we can't help but notice. And because he's willing to "do something, do it over the top, make it more extreme" instead of making a "moderate version," he pushes the limits of unmistakable work with everything he does.

Exposing yourself to a diversity of inputs is like combining spices to make dishes that nobody else could make but you. This turns out to be a powerful accelerant for unmistakable work. Read books apart from your usual genres, listen to music that you might not think would appeal to you, and start to develop your own subconscious database.

Only in our willingness to open ourselves up to a wide variety of cultural and artistic influences, to "avoid moderation, go over the top," and to reach our own extremes do we start to develop an unmistakable signature. The more we do this, the more we pour every bit of who we are into the work we're creating. As Mars says, "it becomes not a conscious effort but a necessity."

Defining Unmistakable

Mars Dorian defines unmistakable as "breaking down every single barrier within your head and truly unleashing that boundless originality that resides within you. That's what I've been trying for the last five years, just cutting one wall after another, until only my essence exists. It's about hacking away the unessential."

PART 5:
THE IMPACT ZONE

In the impact zone, a surfer's love for waves is put to the test and his love affair with the ocean is met with indifference. Anybody who has ever surfed has been in and dealt with the impact zone. The ocean literally beats you on the head with wave after wave after wave. The waves seem like they are never going to stop, like you're never going to come up for air, like you're never going to make it back to the lineup or the shore. You think you're about to drown.

Surf journalist Sam George said: "There are two types of people who surf [the Banzai] Pipeline. Those who have experienced a horrific wipeout there and those who will." If you want to ride epic waves, you have to accept the potential wipeouts.

The impact zone is a fitting metaphor for the darkest chapters of our lives, for what we have to push through in order to create unmistakable work. After hundreds of conversations with people who have become unmistakable masters in their fields, I've found one thing they all have in common is having survived the impact zone. When a founder runs out of money or gets fired from his own start-up, he's in the impact zone. When your film is a dud, nobody comes to your gallery opening, or you lose time and money that can't be recovered, you end up in the impact zone. When we are forced to pull the plug on a project or abandon a dream, we end up in the impact zone.

It would be really nice if we could shield ourselves from adversity, trauma, heartbreak, and all the other negative parts of life. No amount of visualizing, chanting mantras, or repeating affirmations will prepare you for these inevitable experiences. Unfortunately the only way to prepare for the impact zone is to be in it. You have to take some waves on the head so that you're more prepared for the impact zone the next time you end up there.

As my mentor Greg Hartle told me, "The problems don't go away, what changes is your capacity to handle them." As your ability to endure moments in the impact zone increases, you'll be able to ride bigger waves. And as your capacity to handle bigger problems increases, you'll be able to take on bigger creative challenges.

If you're on the path to becoming unmistakable, pushing edges, and charging bigger waves, you're bound to find yourself in the impact zone sooner or later. You will be pushed to your breaking point. As with the surfers who ride epic waves, it's just part of unmistakable work.

MY MOMENT IN THE IMPACT ZONE

By the end of 2014, I had managed to run my company nearly into the ground. I was seriously considering shutting down the *Unmistakable Creative*. The business that had seemed like it was on the edge of massive growth at the beginning of the year had lost its momentum, was hemorrhaging its cash reserve and struggling to generate revenue. It felt more like a sinking ship than an unmistakable movement.

I had let down mentors, friends, and many other people. Greg Hartle had poured tons of his time and energy into me to help take my business to the next level while he was desperately awaiting a potential kidney transplant. I completely isolated myself from and turned my back on the community of friends I'd built because I couldn't handle facing them. When we are not well psychologically, our social interactions don't make sense to anyone. We're not the people they've known and come to love, and trying to live up to their expectations is a daily battle.

I was going to sleep hoping I'd never wake up again and waking up in the middle of the night with heart palpitations.

As I was standing on the top of a hill watching the sunset with my soon-to-be CEO and business partner, Brian Koehn, he told me: "Right now you're the biggest liability to the business." Going from the highs of significant accomplishments to extreme lows in one year had sent me into a spiral of despair. As the founder of a brand known for inspiring people to live better lives, I was suicidal.

That year, 2014, was the most difficult year of my life. It was my impact zone, my test of how badly I wanted to stay in the lineup and surf. My confidence diminished, my stress and anxiety skyrocketed, and I found myself in a vicious cycle in which the struggles of the business began to cause depression, and the depression created more struggles in the business.

Everything compounded. I had lost my confidence and also everyone else's: sponsors didn't renew their contracts and team members had stopped believing in the brand. By the end of the year, what had been a hugely successful event that we had planned to host annually was canceled due to lack of ticket sales. I was pelted by waves, feeling like I would be trapped forever in the impact zone.

These moments test us, mold us, and shape us. But when we're going through them, like surfers taking waves on the head, they seem like they are never going to end. If you're feeling like you can't see which way is up, know that this struggle is part of doing anything that will make you unmistakable. It's temporary. Waves come in sets, and eventually you won't be taking them on the head.

So that begs the question: how did I finally get out of the white water?

Changing the Conversation

At the beginning of 2015, our bank balance indicated that we were losing thousands of dollars each month. Only a year before we'd thought we had a two-year runway, but now we were nine months from bankruptcy and nobody on our team was taking a salary. If we kept going at the current rate, we wouldn't be able to pay our hosting fees or our artists, and we'd have no choice but to shut everything down and declare it a failure. I felt as if everything I'd learned meant nothing and made no difference. I was consumed by a tremendous amount of anxiety and an incredibly debilitating narrative that went like this:

The work I've done in the world has done more harm than good. I'll never be able to find work again. Relationships are ruined because of it. Friendships are damaged. People have lost time and money. If this doesn't work out, I'll have wasted the past seven years of my life. Every critic, every relative who questioned my sanity, will be proven right.

We can easily twist our stories so that all the worst things we think about ourselves seem true. The key to getting out of a dark tunnel is finding even the slightest bit of light.

Every week I would meet with Brian Koehn and start the conversation with "How many more months do we have left until we're out of money?" After about six weeks of this, Brian finally said, "I think it's time for us to change this conversation from how long do we have, to what are we going to do to turn this thing around?"

I realized once again that surfing was the answer. The first step was to get back to the lineup in a literal sense. During this challenging period, the amount of time I was spending in the water had been reduced drastically. At the recommendation of podcast guest Jim Bunch, who told me that the counterintuitive key to a turnaround was filling your days with whatever brings you joy, I made surfing a priority in my life again.

My second step was to go for a small wave to restore my

confidence. Then I could go for more small waves to stabilize and normalize. I started with the smallest wave imaginable: collecting screenshots of tweets and e-mails from people who were benefiting from the *Unmistakable Creative*. When I made the conscious decision to look for them, I started to notice them every day.

Next, I upgraded my environment. I hung framed prints of the *Unmistakable Creative* guests whom I looked up to most. This served multiple purposes. First, it reminded me of all the amazing people with whom I'd had conversations. Second, it was a visual reminder of what these guests had accomplished in their own creative journeys and it gave me something to aspire to. One of the framed prints was of author Sally Hogshead with the caption "How the world sees you at your best." My work was in fact how the world saw me at my best.

I also made it a point to keep a gratitude journal, where I wrote down three things that I was grateful for each day.

I then got ruthless about my daily habits—what time I woke up, what time I went to sleep, and what I ate. Of all the things contributing to my depression, sleep deprivation was at the top of the list. It was a bit of a catch-22: I was depressed because I couldn't get enough sleep, and I couldn't sleep because I was depressed.

So I went to see my doctor, who prescribed medication that would help me sleep. Now taking any kind of medication for mental health carries a stigma in the community I grew up in, as it does in many communities. Seeking help is shrouded in shame, with the stereotype that therapy is for crazy people, and the only acceptable solution is to numb our pain, rather than to talk about it and deal with it. Living with fear, anxiety, and depression bottled up inside is considered more acceptable than seeking help. People keep quiet about their challenges until they're pushed to a breaking point. Occasionally we are woken up to this reality. One of my cousins told me a story about a Silicon Valley engineer who was laid off from his job. The layoff had sent him into a spiral of shame and despair, and rather than get help, even with a wife and kids who would be left behind, he committed suicide. That's how strong the stigma is— we'll choose death over being labeled crazy. But I was desperate enough to give medication a shot, and for the first time in three months I finally slept an entire night all the way through.

Meanwhile, I had discovered that many highly functioning people, CEOs of big companies, successful artists, and many of our guests on the show had dealt with periods of struggle or depression. Nearly all of them had turned to somebody for help. In her book *The Crossroads of Should and Must,* Elle Luna writes: "Our cultural lack of encouragement for psychological health is one of the primary sources of our own unhappiness, dissatisfaction, and deepest inner suffering."

Elle likens seeing a therapist for our mental health to working with a trainer at the gym. In the worst periods of our lives, support systems are essential. Pride or vanity may tempt us to go it alone, but we do so at our own peril. So although I still felt queasy about needing help, I made an appointment to see a therapist.

Unconditional support was the most critical ingredient in my surviving the impact zone. When we are challenging the status quo, we need someone by our side challenging it with us, sharing our vision for what a better future could look like. We need someone to believe in us when we are having a difficult time believing in ourselves. My business partner Brian Koehn played such a critical role in getting me out of the impact zone. Without him I would have drowned. He was not only encouraging, but also kind, and he supported me unconditionally throughout every challenge we faced.

A bad wipeout or an extended period in the impact zone can cause you to feel shell-shocked. The idea of attempting big projects still makes me a bit nervous. But the advantage I have when it comes to the impact zone is that I've already been there. Next time won't be nearly as long, heavy, or harsh. Most important, I have faith that I won't drown because I know how to handle being there.

Grit

Have I mentioned that I have virtually zero natural athletic ability? I was the most improved player on my seventh-grade basketball team (i.e., the worst on the team), and when my friends learned to snowboard in college, I was the only one who couldn't get down a mountain without falling. But I persisted when it came to surfing, and as a result I eventually stood up.

Grit, the willingness to stick with something far past when the average person would quit, is ultimately what will get you past the impact zone and back to the lineup. Grit develops when you continually place yourself in uncomfortable situations and then learn to get comfortable in those spots to emerge on the other side of them with a few scars. By taking a few waves on the head, you develop a tolerance for adversity. The ability to handle situations that once would have caused you a tremendous amount of anxiety becomes your new normal.

But often your temptation to quit is at its highest in the impact zone. When we view anything as our one and only shot at some external marker of success and it doesn't meet our expectations, we set ourselves up for disappointment, debilitating internal narratives, and worrying anxiety. Keep in mind that one work of art, project, or failure doesn't define you. One start-up isn't your only shot at an IPO. One movie isn't your only chance of becoming the next Spielberg. Knowing that we'll always have the option to try again, or try something else, gives us an ability to persist until we manage to get back into the lineup and catch another wave. But the way you learn this is by trying and failing. The impact zone is often what stands between us and the next level of accomplishment.

One of the common threads of the stories on the *Unmistakable Creative* that emerges from people's impact zone experiences is redemption. The impact zone frequently turns out to be the catalyst for significant change in people's lives.

One of the most powerful cases of redemption is the *Unmistakable Creative* guest who served two life sentences in prison. Andy Dixon could be a character in a Martin Scorsese film. He comes from "a long line of people who believed living outside the law was the only way to live." Criminal activity and violence were not only a normal part of his upbringing, they were encouraged and deeply woven into the fabric of his life.

While some kids got praised for straight As with a report card on a refrigerator, Andy was praised for his brutality. When he beat up another kid on the playground and came into the family-owned bar afterward, he was held up on his family members' shoulders. Receiving love and affection for violence he inflicted created a strong imprint early in his life. By the age of ten, he was a member of a gang. By the age of twelve he shot another gang member for the first time. As he grew older, the crime and violence intensified.

Eventually he ended up serving two life sentences. While Andy was in prison, after nearly nine years of continued violence, a priest turned him on to reading books about historical figures like Martin Luther King Jr., Thich Nhat Hanh, and others who had made drastic changes in their lives. These books had a profound influence on Andy, and as a result he decided he was done with violence.

As the AIDS epidemic started hitting prisons, Andy became a health advocate for other prisoners. He also became an adviser to prisoners with disciplinary problems. But a prison staff member told the judge at Andy's parole hearing that he should not receive parole, and his sentence was changed to life without parole. He fought this ruling, and with the help of a lawyer, and his wife, whom he met while in prison, his sentence was reduced. After twenty-seven years, Andy Dixon was released from prison.

After his release, Andy committed his life to helping former inmates find work to keep them from returning to prison. While in prison Andy would see young kids come to visit their parents. Years later he would see those same kids walking the prison yard as inmates, and they would have an uncle and a cousin on the same block. He realized that serving time was a legacy. In some states, incarceration rate forecasts were being based on how many children current prisoners had. So he also established a nonprofit committed to keeping kids with parents in prison from ending up on the same path.

Andy's story illustrates how the impact zone can be turned into something powerful and positive even if we seem doomed, as long as we can pause, reflect, and ask ourselves, "What's the gift in all this?" Believing that redemption will come from it enables us to develop grit.

Cleanup Sets

Sometimes what makes the difference between success and failure is the willingness to stick with an endeavor a bit longer. In his book *The Dip,* Seth Godin writes, "Extraordinary benefits accrue to the tiny minority of people who are able to push just a tiny bit longer than most." When we persist we make invisible progress. We can't see the immediate results of our efforts until much further down the road, but those small steps add up toward our goal. When my business partner Brian founded his skateboard company, he took small daily actions that in the moment didn't seem to be affecting his business. But over two years, they added up to results in the form of twenty-seven stores carrying his skateboards.

I've noticed that the impact zone tends to clear out a crowded lineup. Surfers refer to the waves they're taking on the head when they're in the impact zone as "cleanup" sets. People who don't have the energy, strength, or desire to fight their way through the impact zone and back to the lineup soon abandon the water. You're left with an uncrowded lineup and more waves that are yours for the taking.

In the years that I've been a podcaster, writer, and content creator I've seen a lot of people fall victim to cleanup sets. When they don't see an immediate result from their work, they get out of the water. When I saw a podcaster lamenting on Facebook that he had recorded four episodes of his new show but nobody was listening, writing off podcasting as a waste of time, I recognized another cleanup set victim. As author Todd Henry says, we must have the "grit to persistently do hard things that have no immediate payoff."

We admire persistence when someone succeeds, but do not encourage it when that person struggles. This is even truer as we become older. Actor Ethan Hawke said, "When you're younger everyone tells you to follow your dreams. When you get older they get offended if you even try." When we're persistent we have to believe and be able to see what doesn't currently exist. If the outcome from our efforts is guaranteed, by definition it's not unmistakable, because someone else has already done it.

No quest to become unmistakable will be devoid of time in the impact zone and the necessity to persist, because the pursuit of significant feats invites significant challenges into our lives. Those who can persist through the impact zone are the ones who become unmistakable. In fact, persistence reveals elements of what makes us unmistakable. Our first, second, and third attempts at anything may cause us to end up in the impact zone. But when we persist, we are able to return to the lineup with experience and wisdom that we didn't have before. Once we know what works for us, we have a filter for making decisions differently, for when we should go for a wave, and when we should wait for the next one.

Billionaire venture capitalist Chris Sacca said, "You'll never feel richer than when your net worth is zero," to describe his moment in the impact zone. His Lowercase Capital investments now include Twitter, Instagram, and Uber, but in 1998 he started a hedge fund with his student loan money. Within eighteen months it had made $12 million. Then in the spring of 2000 he lost it all in one week, putting him $4 million in debt. What followed were five years of persistence and grit that eventually led him to a net worth of zero dollars. And continued persistence paid off even more because today, Chris Sacca is a billionaire. Sacca's story teaches us that the bigger the waves we attempt to ride, the heavier the waves on our head will be when we're in the impact zone.

Our moments in the impact zone are not always financial or professional setbacks. In many cases they're deeply personal.

Jennifer Boykin, a frequent contributor to online publications including *The Huffington Post,* is the creator of the global community Life After Tampons, a midlife reinvention move-ment for women. Her time in the impact zone started with a tragedy that for most of us is unfathomable: the loss of her first child. But as she reflected on an episode of the *Unmistakable Creative*:

> *When it comes to loss or failure or anything where you feel like the force is disturbed in the universe, all you need to do is look around not too far, and you'll see other people who have their hardships as well, and maybe you wouldn't exchange yours for that. Our sorrow can be the gateway to our freedom and we can choose to get bitter or better.*

A year or two after the death of her daughter, Jennifer did a workshop for her church about healing from loss. Within six months she found her calling as a speaker, but it was prior to the existence of the Internet, so she didn't have an easy way to build a platform. Her sons were still at home and she put the dream of speaking on hold. She then got a master's degree in writing at a university where a Pulitzer Prize–winning profes-sor told her she was the best student he'd ever had. But she didn't continue writing because "when we meet the enormity of what could be possible for us we get afraid."

On her fiftieth birthday she decided it was now or never. She started Life After Tampons and transformed her loss into an act of service for women around the world. Jennifer's story teaches us that even the most catastrophic of losses can open us to significant personal growth and create an opportunity to ride the kinds of waves that might never have been possible without such loss, grief, and redemption. While we will inevitably look back and wonder what life might have been like had things been different, we must also consider what people and experiences would not be part of our lives today if things had gone exactly as we thought they should.

Sometimes confronting our mortality and ending up in the impact zone can serve as a difficult but necessary wake-up call. Our first instinct and natural human reaction in our impact zone moments is not to accept it and embrace our setbacks or failures. We want to panic and imagine worst-case scenarios. We often choose to get bitter before we get better. At just the thought of an incurable disease, you might want to get your affairs in order and start planning for the worst. But this is our true test: in the most frightening impact zone moments, we can prepare to die or truly start to live.

What if we could see our moment in the impact zone as a necessary loss, which serves as a catalyst for making significant change in our lives? I'm not saying not to grieve, cry, or acknowledge your pain. Many of our losses are absolutely devastating. But the greatest gifts emerge from periods of greatest pain. When we reach the point of no return with nothing to lose, that can be powerful. Grieve, and when you start to surface, realize that you can make a drastic change from the pain you've endured.

Of all the people I've interviewed, one has endured more time in the impact zone than anyone else I've met. At a young age, my mentor Greg Hartle was abandoned by his father. He grew up in extreme poverty, with almost no furniture, and shared a room with his two siblings. Like Andy Dixon, he turned to crime. He was a gang member, sold drugs, and watched his best friend die in a drive-by shooting.

At age nineteen, Greg had an opportunity to overcome his childhood disadvantages when a couple who co-owned a book-keeping business hired him. They included him in everything from dealing with attorneys and real estate agents to managing finances. They never demanded or directed, but invited him to participate. His boss would leave books on his desk, which he eventually read. From all that he learned there, Greg was able to start his own voice and data communications company.

But his time in the impact zone was far from over. At the age of twenty-five, after having built his business and achieved significant financial success, he was diagnosed with a terminal kidney illness. He was given six months to live unless he could get a kidney transplant. Fortunately his mother turned out to be a perfect match and donated a kidney. While he regained his health, he lost his business and nearly all of his money. He was forced to rebuild from scratch.

From his personal experience of starting over, and also the toll the recession of 2008 and 2009 took on people, he committed three years to helping people rebuild their businesses. Then he found himself yet again in the impact zone. The kidney transplant he had received eleven years prior was failing, and in November 2013 he was given nine months to live. Although he hasn't received a kidney transplant yet, through dialysis he has managed to stay alive as of this writing.

Despite all this, he has a powerful perspective: "Your temporary circumstances don't have to become your permanent identity."

Our time in the impact zone is temporary. Waves come in sets, and the ones we're taking on the head will eventually stop. But our moments in the impact zone can either inform us or define us.

When you've lived through the impact zone, you come out of it with scars. And those scars are not representations just of your most challenging moments. They're also layers that shield you, a shell of sorts. What once would have cracked you now bounces off you. Your shell hardens, but your heart softens.

Unmistakable Creative: Janelle Hanchett

When Janelle Hanchett reunited with her children after several years of separation, she started to question the way the media depicts the parenting experience, wondering if she was the only one who could not identify with that portrayal. As Janelle says, "We've got this fatal flaw that is our humanity. We aren't perfect. This idea that we're going to always have this best self that we put forward to our kids, and result in this great outcome, it's bullshit." Her blog Renegade Mothering, *her "fight against helpful parenting advice," was the result. With 35,000 Facebook fans, 20,000 subscribers, and conversations with literary agents about a potential book, Hanchett has found an unexpected following.*

Latter-day Saints and LSD

Growing up simultaneously attending the Mormon church every week and going on road trips with her mother to see the Grateful Dead, Janelle describes her childhood as "growing up with Jesus and LSD side by side." The roots of her ability to write raw and uncensored material go back to when someone at church handed her a journal and encouraged her to write in it. Reflecting on her early writing, Janelle says, "I learned to write whatever I was thinking, without any fear or repercussion of somebody reading it. I don't know if I was born with a lack of censor. At my core, I couldn't understand why I would ever change who I am to appeal to somebody else. I developed a voice."

By writing as though our work will never be read, without any fear of the repercussions, like Janelle we can start to tap into what our honest, authentic voice actually sounds like. A journal is yours alone, and what you choose to share with the world from it is entirely up to you.

From Drinking to Writing

Like many unmistakables, Janelle's path to discovering what made her unmistakable wasn't free of obstacles and tragedy. By eighteen she was a daily drinker, and from there she became a "hopeless, worthless alcoholic," in and out of institutions and treatment centers. Eventually she hit bottom.

The fact of the matter is I died. I had absolutely nothing left. The only way I can describe it is that the bottle killed me. I woke up on March 5, 2009, and I knew without a shadow of a doubt that I had no moves left. I didn't care if my mom or my kids or my husband came back. I would have given anything to just live one day sober. I was able to get some help and I haven't had a drink since.

With nothing left to lose, she was able to write the truth about herself and her failures as a parent and as a person: "If somebody's going to tell me I'm a bad mother, that I did drugs and breastfed my child, you think I don't fucking know that? Yet I'm here and I'm good, but I don't have anything to prove. Failure was the greatest thing. It was from that place that I started writing."

Hitting rock bottom can be a place of power if you are able to reframe it that way. When you've quite literally got nothing to lose, your life becomes a blank canvas, a place from which you can create anything.

The Start of a No-Bullshit Blog

Reflecting on her experience of being reunited with her children and parenthood was the spark for Janelle's developing an unmistakable voice among myriad "mom blogs":

I was having a good time and really grateful for these kids on a level that I couldn't possibly put into words. Yet I wanted to kill myself half the time I was with them. It wasn't glorious. It wasn't interesting. It wasn't glamorous. Why do all these fucking people act like they know what they're doing? I started having this sneaking suspicion that everybody was full of shit.

So I said, "Screw it! I'm going to write a blog and say the exact truth of my experience exactly how I see it. I'm not going to make it consistent. I'm not going to make it pretty. I'm just going to write it the way it is for me." I really wanted to know if there were other women who felt this way. That's how it started. I can still write as if I had no audience because I just don't give a shit, because of life experiences.

The uncensored truth is a commitment to a bold and compelling point of view. As author Justine Musk once said, "If you're going to have a bold and compelling point of view, you're going to piss some people off." While this might cause your work to be polarizing, it will also make it unmistakable.

We face a natural temptation when we reveal our work in public to hold back, play it safe, and avoid the raw, vulnerable, honest truth of who we are. We filter our voices out of fear that we will be judged or criticized. We sugarcoat the truth. Only when we resist this temptation, when we say what other people are thinking but might not have the courage to say, our voice, like Janelle's, becomes unmistakable.

Defining Unmistakable

Janelle Hanchett describes unmistakable this way: "I think everybody's got something to say, whether it's through their work or through their art or through being a mom or a dad. Figuring out what story you have to tell, and stripping away all the judgment surrounding that, saying, 'Fuck it,' and owning what you are, however small you think it is. I've got friends who are amazing, crafty stay-at-home moms. That authenticity is so powerful, whether you're an amazing knitter or you're super into music. You're witnessing something gorgeous and profound, somebody who's just who they are, and that's what makes people unmistakable."

PART 6: THE STOKE

In my best surf sessions, I lose count of the waves I've caught. Time seems to stand still and fly by all at once. My awareness of every detail, the sparkle of the sunlight off the foam, the pelicans gliding over each wave, the sound of the water and the dolphins swimming by, is heightened. The past and the future dissolve, and the only thought in my mind is how there's no place I'd rather be. This is what I live for. This is my inner compass. This is why I surf. I'm stoked.

This is the feeling that has kept me paddling out, navigating the lineup, risking the drop, and enduring the inevitable moments in the impact zone since I stood up on my first wave in Brazil. The stoke is an unspoken understanding among those of us who surf, who have experienced this mysterious and blissful rite of passage when we feel the thrill of riding waves. In these moments we realize that surfing isn't about the number of waves we catch, but the joy that comes from those we do. As even the most accomplished surfers say: the best surfer in the world is the one having the most fun.

The greatest achievement in surfing is being a "soul surfer." In his essay "The Seven Levels of Surfers," author Thomas Mitchell explains:

> *This is the highest level, the pinnacle of surfing spirituality equivalent to Nirvana, Satori, Total Enlightenment, etc., and*

is rarely attained. The Soul Surfer expresses himself through his unity with the breaking wave. He borrows the wave's spirit for a short while and uses his body and equipment to translate the essence of the wave's spirit into Art. Other Surfers respond to this and immediately recognize the Soul Surfer whether they admit it or not.

Surfers are on a continuum. There are those who push the boundaries of what's possible and there are those who will be completely satisfied surfing six-foot waves for the rest of our lives. In the documentary *Step into Liquid,* journalist and surfing legend Pete Townend said:

The analogy is music. You can have a jazz musician and a rock musician and a classical musician. They each understand and appreciate each other, what that other guy hears, but it's not necessarily their trip. Surfing is the same way.

I believe this feeling is what keeps all creators creating—why musicians keep singing, actors keep acting, entrepreneurs keep building companies, and artists keep making art. The process of creating becomes their oxygen supply. Without it they would die.

Reaching this point in our quest to become unmistakable is magical. Our craft becomes effortless. We find so much joy in what we're doing that we dare greatly and create with a profound sense of optimism. Where others see limitations, we see possibility. Where they see dead ends, we see detours, new destinations to discover, waves that have yet to be surfed.

THE TRUE GIFT OF UNMISTAKABLE

In his 2012 commencement speech, which went viral and eventually became the basis for his book *Make Good Art,* author Neil Gaiman writes:

> *I don't know that it's an issue for anybody but me, but it's true that nothing I did where the only reason for doing it was the money was ever worth it, except as bitter experience. Usually I didn't wind up getting the money, either. The things I did because I was excited, and wanted to see them exist in reality, have never let me down, and I never regretted the time I spent on any of them.*

When an artist reaches a point in his work when what he's seeking can't be quantified or measured by standard metrics like monetary compensation, Web site traffic, and attention from other people, he transcends himself and his work. Creation becomes its own reward, and he becomes a soul surfer.

When my own quest to become unmistakable started, I couldn't imagine planning conferences, leading a creative team, and overseeing a complex media production. Once you experience what it's like to have an expanded sense of possibility, you can't see the world any other way. You couldn't go back if you wanted to. For me, unmistakable isn't being just a brand. It's the filter through which I see the world.

Entrepreneur and author Derek Sivers told me that he saw

entrepreneurship not as an opportunity to make money, but as an opportunity for personal development. He sold his company CD Baby for a small fortune and donated all of it to charity.

The true gift of unmistakable is not what you get, but who you become as a result. Your work turns into something that will never let you down.

The Continuum of Unmistakable

The economy that we are moving toward is one in which we no longer have to follow a set of rules designed to lead us to a predetermined outcome. When the work we're doing can be easily replicated, repeated, scaled, and passed off to the lowest bidder, it's eventually going to be outsourced or eliminated. There's never been a better time to commit to the pursuit of becoming unmistakable.

Unlike any other time in history, we have tools, technology, and the ability to tell our stories, build companies, create personal art projects, and start things that have the potential to become unmistakable. Access to information and education continues to be democratized. For example, the esteemed start-up incubator Y Combinator recently made the class its founders teach at Stanford accessible to the entire world via iTunes.

Every single one of us has at our fingertips the opportunity to create and contribute in unmistakable ways. To determine the worth of our contribution to the world solely based on external markers of success, validation, and accolades is to diminish the value we can create. The value we create can be measured in so many different ways: smiles we put on people's faces, personal growth, professional growth, and more.

Every time we create something that didn't exist before, we change the world. By definition, the act of creating makes the world different from how it was before your creation came into existence. You've probably already changed the world more times than you are aware of—and have the possibility to leave your mark even more.

I've had countless people who listen to our podcast tell me how it's made them more productive and happier in life and at their jobs. Some have quit their jobs and started businesses as a result of our work. Others have started personal art projects they have been thinking about for years—writing books, starting blogs, making short films, and founding charitable groups.

Touching lives in a meaningful and unmistakable way is now accessible to all of us.

Leaving Your Heart Onstage

The stage will be different for each of us. Mine has taken the form of blank pages, podcasts, and literal stages. Yours may take the form of a company, movie, kitchen, or something else. Whatever form that stage takes, you have a chance to leave your heart on it and hold nothing back; leave the world something to remember you by, with an offering of projects and pieces of art that are unmistakably yours.

In October 2003, author Patti Digh's stepfather was diagnosed with lung cancer. He died thirty-seven days later. This loss led her to create her Web site 37days.com, driven by the question "What would I be doing with my life if I only had 37 days to live?" The loss of her stepfather was a moment in which she came to a profound realization:

> We act as if we have all the time in the world—that's not a new understanding. But the definiteness of 37 days struck me. So short a time, as if all the regrets of a life would barely have time to register before time was up.

Up until that point she'd been a business author. Now she wanted to "write like hell, leave as much of myself behind for my two daughters as I could, let them know me and see me as a real person, not just a mother, leave with them for safe-keeping my thoughts and memories, fears and dreams, the histories of what I am and who my people are."

The blog was her stage, and she left her heart on it via her words.

You have the opportunity to leave your heart on whatever stage you choose. To waste that chance would be to miss out on changing the world.

To leave your heart onstage is to put everything you have into every last ounce of your work. You commit to avoiding mediocrity at all costs, and make sure your blood, sweat, tears, and DNA are infused into your work. You commit to creating something that people will never forget. You might hate the process, but you'll love the result.

We might get to do certain projects only once in a lifetime. When we leave our hearts onstage, we become aware that every time we do something it could be the last time. We're all dying, just at varying rates. We must ask ourselves one simple question that will enable us to increase the odds of our work's being unmistakable:

> *If I was never going to be in this exact situation again, what would I do? How would I show up if "This is it?"*

The question is not about just your business or your art, it's about how you live every aspect of your life. To leave your heart onstage is to commit to an unmistakable standard. I can't help but wonder if Michael Jackson had a premonition about his death when he declared "This is it" during his final curtain call. If you watch the documentary about how he prepared for his final concert tour, one thing is very clear: Michael was committed to leaving his heart onstage, and he saw his performance as his gift to the world. He defines unmistakable.

I once heard that a book is the start of a conversation between two people. It is my hope that this is not the end, but a new beginning for you and me. Unmistakable isn't about creating labels to identify with because labels limit your capacity. It's about shedding them, until what's left is a limitless, no-bullshit version of who you are: unmistakable.

Unmistakable Creative: Seth Godin

To uncover what makes you unmistakable, you must be willing to question how things are done and attempt to change them. Seth Godin has made a career out of questioning the way things are done across multiple disciplines ranging from business to publishing to education. He doesn't simply question, however. He continually experiments with change and improvements. Seth's willingness to keep trying things that might not work, to be wrong or criticized, to stand out instead of fit in, is what makes him unmistakable. The author of eighteen books, including Tribes, Purple Cow, *and* Linchpin, *he writes a popular daily blog. His books are international bestsellers, translated into more than thirty-five languages. He's also the founder of Squidoo, a Web site platform that allowed users to create pages called lenses, zooming in on areas of expertise.*

Something That Begs to Be Shared

In the summer of 2014 Seth invited people to his office for a free weeklong seminar, and he found himself talking about both the internal and external forces that make unmistakable work happen more specifically than he had before, which was the impetus for his book What to Do When It's Your Turn. *By combining images, short sentences, and* material that felt like blog posts in a format that would appeal to people who don't read books, he realized he'd developed a tool that he and his fans could use to change those around them.

If "the only books most people read are books that other people give them," the question you might raise in your efforts to become unmistakable is "How do I write a book that people will be tempted to give to others?" Built into that question are the unspoken questions of how you'll know you're right and how to avoid being wrong. History has proven, time and again, that people have been wrong about art that changes our culture.

Half of Bob Dylan's fifty albums are below average for Bob Dylan. He writes "Lay, Lady, Lay," or he comes out with an album that changes the culture, and then ten years go by when it's not resonating with people. Does that mean he says, "I'm going to make no albums?" Almost every bestseller is a surprise bestseller. Almost every movie that breaks box-office records was declined by a studio before it came out. Almost every critic has been wrong repeatedly about the books and the ideas that changed our lives.

If all we do is continually try to avoid being wrong, we'll never be able to do work that's unmistakable. If, on the other hand, we seek out opportunities to fail, learn from, and iterate on those failures, we increase the likelihood of creating art that changes our culture and ideas that change people's lives.

Managing Fear, Resistance, and Our Critics

"This might not work" has been an essential part of Seth's ethos and creative style. When we do things that might not work we expose ourselves to the possibility of failure, but we also increase the likelihood of creating unmistakable work.

In addition to writing books, Seth has written more than seven thousand blog posts. Producing such a high volume of output has enabled him to continually refine his craft. When I asked him about how we overcome our immediate temptation not to try again after we fail, he said:

> The only way you learn how to walk is by not walking, not walking, falling, not walking, falling, walking a little, falling, walking a lot, falling, walking. There's a long history of every successful person who's changed anything beginning with them learning how to walk where they didn't give up.

To do unmistakable work, you'll have to embrace Seth's notion of not walking, falling, walking, not giving up, and walking. What Seth's creative process teaches is the tremendous power that comes with our willingness to show up and make something every day. If you plotted anyone's path to become unmistakable on a graph, it's never a line going straight up and to the right; it's a series of ups and downs.

Wrestling with our fear, failure, resistance, obstacles, and setbacks is an inevitable part of doing unmistakable work. Whether you're a bestselling author like Seth or somebody who is just getting started, fear will always be with you. The most revealing insight on fear that he shared with me was: "The enemy of creativity is fear; that seems pretty clear. The enemy of fear is creativity; that doesn't seem that obvious." The antidote to our fear is to put our heads down, do our work, and make something each day.

We also have the power to insulate ourselves from debilitating internal monologues. One of the reasons that Seth has intentionally chosen not to have comments on his blog is because "hearing negative feedback from anonymous people who I have no connection with will cause me to do nothing but hide."

When we concede our power to a critic, by making it possible for them to attack us publicly, we end up hiding and sabotaging our best work. Even though the Web has connected us, it's also given us the opportunity to choose whom we want to be connected to and to be deliberate about it. There are two types of critics: the supporters who believe in your work and who give feedback legitimately to help you improve, and the ones who simply are vindictive. An encounter with a critic is an opportunity to make a decision about whom our work is for and whom it's not for. We can either attempt to appease a critic or decide that our work is not for them, and do it for the people who appreciate it.

Will You Choose Cog or Creative?

"In the economy we are in now, if you choose to be a creative, you cannot wait to be picked because the Internet is an amplifier of people who pick themselves," says Seth.

One of the greatest challenges we face to become unmistakable is to let go of our cultural need to be "picked." That need is so baked into our internal narrative because it's what we've been taught to believe for the entirety of our lives.

- We were picked or not to be in honors classes.
- We were picked or not to be the prom king or queen.
- We were picked or not to work at Google, Facebook, or (insert a famous company of your choice).

But to let go of the need to be picked means that we assume a greater level of responsibility in our lives. It means we own our failures and our successes.

At the end of 2015, our team at the Unmistakable Creative compiled a list of one hundred insanely interesting people you should know. We made the list to reject the tyranny of being picked because we'd never been on lists like the Forbes "30 Under 30" or Fast Company's "Most Creative People in Business." Every year when the lists were published we felt a tinge of envy, so we decided to create our own list. The paradox of making such a list, of which the whole purpose was to celebrate the notion that we don't need to get picked, was that people responded with the desire to be on the list next time we made it. One friend told me, "It wouldn't have mattered who made the list. I could have made the list and people would have wanted to be on it." That's how deep our cultural need to be picked runs. And yet it's only in letting go of that need that we're able to do interesting and unmistakable work.

Defining Unmistakable

Seth Godin defines unmistakable this way: "The path to become unmistakable is the willingness to be wrong, to be criticized, and most of all to matter. If you're willing to do something that matters, you are likely to be in the minority. It probably means you're doing something that's unmistakable."

CONCLUSION

An Unmistakable Movement

When a system has failed us, we can air our grievances, protest against it, and fight a losing battle. Or we can make a choice to dismantle that system, disregard its rules, and recreate it to our own liking. Hopefully you're inspired to pursue the second option to embark on your own path to being unmistakable.

The education system and following convention failed me in many ways. The burning desire to reshape that path of convention and conformity—and to expose the alternative choices that people within the boundaries of such a path rarely realize—has been the driving force of my work.

The Unmistakable Creatives I've noted throughout this book have been a source not just of inspiration, but of education. They're our unmistakable teachers and messengers. They equip and inspire us to create unmistakable work, as well as a future that is abundant, one in which the potential of our humanity is pushed to limits far beyond what we might imagine possible today.

Being unmistakable is an opportunity to leave "a trail of magic," as Seth Godin put it, from starting an online publishing project like a blog, podcast, YouTube channel, or portfolio of creative work to building an app or starting a company. You have no limits, only perceptions of limitation that are more imagined than real, more fiction than fact.

FOUR IDEAS TO START YOUR UNMISTAKABLE MOVEMENT

Author Derek Sivers says that "the first follower is what trans-forms a lone nut into a leader." The result is the beginning of a movement. All of us start becoming unmistakable as lone nuts. But the quest isn't about just ourselves or products and services; it's about starting a movement by doing work that people can't help but be drawn to and want to be a part of. These four ideas about how to start a movement are intentionally simple be-cause there's no map, just a compass:

1) **Buy a notebook and jot down all your ideas.** You'll plant seeds for some of your life's most unmistakable work here. Seven Moleskine notebooks ago I was mapping out a book based on surfing metaphors.

2) **Build a basic Web site to serve as your HQ.** A Web site is your platform for sharing ideas, art, whatever you can't help but want to share. It will be ground zero for your movement. The act of creating your virtual home will start to take on a life of its own, and lead you to places you've never been and waves that you can't imagine surfing right now.

3) **Make a list of people you want to meet or connect with.** Find the Web sites and online profiles of people who inspire you and research them. Get to know them and what makes them tick and matters most to them. Many people have said that you become the average of the five people you surround

yourself with. Fortunately, on the Internet you're in complete control of whom you choose. Every week reach out to one of those people and write down a lesson you've learned from your research.

4) **Share your movement.** Whether you've started a blog, or you're posting paintings on Instagram, building a company, or making movies, share your movement. If you're using social media, use the hashtag #unmistakable so we can share in this movement together!

USING YOUR .1 PERCENT

When I started my quest to become unmistakable in 2009, I was at a crossroads between a life that was deliberate, creative, and filled with adventure, a life spent doing my own work that truly mattered to me, versus following someone else's script, living by a predetermined set of rules, and worst of all, living an average life at a level of continuous mediocrity.

The end of a book is the start of a new chapter—your personal crossroads. If you've made it this far, you clearly have the yearning to become unmistakable. It might be a spark that needs to be ignited or a calling that has been drowned out by the noise of judgments, expectations, fear, and self-doubt. But underneath it all is a unique combination of experiences, perspective, and the ability to contribute to the world what nobody else can but you.

I recently read in a science journal that human beings are almost identical in terms of the 99.9 percent of DNA we all share. So what will you do with the .1 percent of you that has never existed before and will never exist again? How will you use your singular .1 percent of individuality to become an unmistakable creative?

The pursuit of unmistakable is a commitment to live a life that is deliberate, a life that is filled with intention, meaning, and purpose.

A life in which you embrace the notion that you were born to create.

A life in which you are unapologetically yourself, and you turn the volume up to 10 on who you are and how you show up in the world.

A life in which you unequivocally know quite literally the future is, always has been, and always will be unwritten and uncertain, a blank canvas that is yours to be shaped into an unmistakable masterpiece.

A life in which the rules get redefined and the borders and boundaries of possibility are not just stretched, but pushed to the limits of your potential.

Let your compass guide you to unexplored shores and waves you've never surfed. Go to the point of no return. Let the idea of unmistakable seep into your bones, into your blood, every breath you take, every word you put down on a page, and every work of art you make. Rewrite the story of your life in a way that nobody else could but you, filled with your humanity, your willingness not to play it safe, and your willingness not to hold back. Let it become so deeply embedded it's not something you do, it's who you are—and every single thing you touch inevitably will become unmistakable.

Creation is its own reward. Unmistakable work is what the world deserves. So charge each wave with everything you've got, go make something unmistakable, paddle back out to the lineup, take a deep breath, and do it again. You were born to be unmistakable.

ACKNOWLEDGMENTS

To Stephanie Frerich, thank you for believing in the idea of *Unmistakable* and helping to bring it to life.

Lisa DiMona, my agent, you're a true rock star, and I'm so grateful to have you in my life.

Robin Dellabough, you've been more than an editor and writing coach. You've been a true mentor and friend, never sugarcoating your feedback and holding me to incredibly high standards.

Brian Koehn, you're not just a business partner and a best friend, but a brother. I wouldn't have made it through the impact zone without your encouraging me to get back to the lineup.

Derek Wyatt, you've continually taught me to consider the balance between art and commerce.

Greg Hartle, the impact you've had on my life has been nothing short of profound. I wouldn't be here without your guidance and mentorship. Thanks for constantly pushing me to do work where I might have hated the process but loved the result.

Sid Savara, if you hadn't sent me that e-mail years ago, the *Unmistakable Creative* might not exist.

Mike Harrington, thanks for being a daily confidant and holding me accountable.

Mars Dorian, you define what it means to create art that requires no signature. It's been a gift to collaborate with you for all these years.

Thanks to AJ Leon for teaching me to think like an artist and be deliberate with every single thing I've done.

Charmaine Haworth, thank you for always making me feel my best when I was at my worst.

Matthew Monroe, thank you for kicking my ass when I wanted to quit.

And to the hundreds of guests who have appeared on our show over the past several years, all of this has been made possible by your guidance and generosity.

To my mom, dad, and sister, thank you for enduring the years of uncertainty and choices that on occasion probably made you wonder what I was thinking, and for letting me use the library at our house as Unmistakable HQ.

UNMISTAKABLE RESOURCES

Numerous authors, thinkers, and creators have shaped my work, my habits, and my perspective on the idea of what it means to be unmistakable. Below is a list of books, blogs, podcasts, movies, tools, and even a few surf spots to assist you in your own quest to become unmistakable.

Books

#GIRLBOSS by Sophia Amoruso

The 4-Hour Chef by Timothy Ferris

A Beautiful Mind by Sylvia Nasar

Bold by Peter Diamandis and Steven Kotler

Creativity Inc. by Ed Catmull and Amy Wallace

The Crossroads of Should and Must by Elle Luna

Daily Rituals by Mason Currey

Deep Work by Cal Newport

The Dip, What to Do When It's Your Turn, and *The Icarus Deception* by Seth Godin

The Fire Starter Sessions by Danielle LaPorte

The Happiness Advantage by Shawn Achor

I Am Malala by Malala Yousafzai and Christina Lamb

The Impact Equation by Chris Brogan and Julien Smith

The Leap Year Project by Victor Said

Life Is a Verb by Patti Digh

Little Bets by Peter Sims

Louder Than Words by Todd Henry

Make Good Art by Neil Gaiman

The Man Who Outgrew His Prison Cell by Joe Loya

Mastery and *The 48 Laws of Power* by Robert Greene

The Mesh by Lisa Gansky

A Million Miles in a Thousand Years and *Scary Close* by Donald Miller

No Baggage by Clara Bensen

The Obstacle Is the Way by Ryan Holiday

Orange Is the New Black by Piper Kerman

Outliers by Malcolm Gladwell

Quitter and *Do Over* by Jon Acuff

Rejection Proof by Jia Jiang

The Rise of Superman by Steven Kotler

Shadow Divers by Robert Kurson

SoulPancake by Rainn Wilson, Devon Gundry, Golriz Lucina, and Shabnam Mogharabi

Steal Like an Artist by Austin Kleon

Talent Is Overrated by Geoff Colvin

Think Like a Stripper by Erika Lyremark

Uncertainty by Jonathan Fields

Unthink by Erik Wahl

The War of Art by Steven Pressfield

What the Most Successful People Do Before Breakfast by Laura Vanderkam

Movies, Documentaries, and YouTube Videos

A Beautiful Mind

Chris Sacca's commencement speech at the Carlson School of Management: https://www.youtube.com/watch?v=RskzY HPlh5U

Coach Carter: A great example of how deliberate practice impacts performance and talent.

Demetri Martin's comedic sketch on life coaching: http://www.cc.com/video-clips/9nppso/the-daily-show-with-jon-stewart-trendspotting---life-coaching

Jiro Dreams of Sushi: A must watch for anyone who wants to truly understand what it takes and what it means to master your craft.

Kid President by Brad Montague: http://www.kidpresident.com

Private Parts: The story of Howard Stern's radio career.

SoulPancake videos: http://www.youtube.com/user/soul pancake

Step Into Liquid: A documentary by filmmaker Dana Brown that profiles surfers from all over the globe and all walks of life. There's no better introduction to the world of surfing for a non-surfer.

The Tim Ferriss Experiment

Unmistakable Creative Shorts: The animated series produced with SoulPancake. http://bit.ly/ucshorts

Blogs, Podcasts, Web sites, and Tools

37days.com by Patti Digh: http://www.37days.com

Black Girls Code: http://www.blackgirlscode.com

"Blog Mastermind" by Yaro Starak: http://www.blogmaster mind.com

"The Craziest OkCupid Date Ever," by Clara Bensen: http://www.salon.com/2013/11/12/the_craziest_okcupid_date _ever

Exile Lifestyle by Colin Wright: http://www.exilelifestyle.com

The Experience Institute by Victor Saad: http://expinsti tute.com

Fearbuster.com by Jia Jiang: http://www.fearbuster.com

How to Start a Startup: https://startupclass.co

The Instigator Experience: http://www.instigatordev.com

Life After Tampons by Jennifer Boykin: http://www.lifeafter tampons.com

The Life and Times of a Remarkable Misfit: http://aj-leon .com/pursuitofeverything/the-life-and-times-of-a-remark able-misfits

MarsDorian.com: http://www.marsdorian.com

MastermindTalks podcast with Jayson Gaignard: http://www .mmtpodcast.com

The Middle Finger Project: http://www.themiddlefingerpro ject.org

One Month: Learn how to code Web sites, build apps, and grow your business. http://www.onemonth.com

PageCloud: An easy-to-use Web site builder. http://pagecloud.com

Renegade Mothering: The fight against meaningful parenting advice. http://www.renegademothering.com

Seth Godin's blog: http://sethgodin.typepad.com

Sitecast: Another Web site building tool that *Unmistakable Creative* is built upon. https://sitecast.com

Off Camera with Sam Jones: http://offcamera.com. In particular, Ethan Hawke on the *Off Camera* podcast: http://offcam era.com/issues/ethan-hawke/watch/#.VzNMaLeFNEY

The Ultimate Game of Life by Jim Bunch: http://www.theulti mategameoflife.com

Unmistakable Creative: For access to interviews with all the *Unmistakable Creative* guests mentioned in this book. http://unmistakablecreative.com/book

"Why Should Anyone Read Your Blog?" by Sonia Simone: http://www.copyblogger.com/why-read-your-blog

WTF with Marc Maron podcast: http://www.wtfpod.com

Surf-related Resources

The K-Lodge El Salvador Surf Camp: If you're looking for a few days of royal treatment and great waves, you can't go wrong with Walter Torres, who owns this place. Part of this book was written at the K-Lodge. http://elsalvadorsurfcamp.net

Outsite: A new kind of co-working facility, where you can stay, work, and play in beautiful places. Be sure to check out their San Diego location if you want to mix in some work and surf. http://outsite.co

"The Seven Levels of Surfers" by Thomas Mitchell: http://www.kenrockwell.com/tech/7surf.htm

Witch's Rock Surf Camp, Tamarindo, Costa Rica: Warm water, beachfront lodging, and great waves make this one of the best places in the world to learn how to surf. http://witchs rocksurfcamp.com

CONNECTING TO UNMISTAKABLE HQ

Visit UnmistakableCreative.com/book for access to interviews with all the people I've mentioned and additional bonus material.

Follow us on Twitter: @unmistakableCR.

Find us on Facebook: www.facebook.com/unmistakable creative.